BAGHA JATIN:
THE REVOLUTIONARY LEGACY

BAGHA JATIN: THE REVOLUTIONARY LEGACY

Dr. Prithwindra Mukherjee

Indus Source Books

Indian Spirit, Universal Wisdom

Indus Source Books
PO Box 6194
Malabar Hill PO
Mumbai 400 006
INDIA
Email: info@industsource.com
www.indussource.com

Bagha Jatin: The Revolutionary Legacy

Published in India by
Indus Source Books, Mumbai.

ISBN 13: 978-81-88569-72-4

First Published 2015.

Photos courtesy: *Les racines intellectuelles du mouvement d'indépendance de l'Inde* by Prithwindra Mukherjee
Editions Codex, France, 2010.

Cover design by Sanskruti Graphics, Mumbai

Printed at Repro India Ltd., Mumbai.

CONTENTS

PREFACE

An eminent Bengali historian and sociologist has pertinently claimed Rammohun Roy (1772-1833) to have been the mouthpiece of the awakening Indian elite in the nineteenth century.[1] This very elite, according to him—towards the bend of the century—was to take a militant turn. Point by point, an indomitable merit-centred will to contest with the pragmatic colonial power in all walks of life got the upper hand while an overall blossoming of their "Indianity" was progressively confirmed. On one side, a host of personalities towering in their genius and tempered by paradoxical claims of Reason and Revelation, on the other hand followed, however, rules of dialectics all over the country, striving towards a synthesis. Impetuous in their urge to expand, to shatter all limitations and taboos, once for all, the Indian elite discerned in British imperialism the greatest impediment to the spontaneous fulfilment of its secret objective. Sociologists believe that a revolution has to begin first of all in the people's psychology, before its phase of exploding on the material plane. Mutually conflicting ideas and ideals proved to intensify young India's existential aspirations.

Foremost among those pioneers, Swami Vivekananda—shortly before his passing, in 1902—, is said to have anticipated bombs for India's cause.[2] During an evening party in Paris, it is reported that he had requested Emma Calvé, the famous soprano star, to sing for him *La Marseillaise*, the French national anthem. Furious against such a proposal, when someone protested—condemning the song to be warlike, with cannons thundering and soldiers roaring—the Swami had replied immediately: "That is what I want. Have you not heard the heroic accent in every line of this hymn, the passionate patriotic call to sacrifice everything? Don't you sense, on hearing it, the way it incites the stunned and sceptical mass to stand up? This is the hymn that I want all my followers to learn."[3] Does it not remind us how—at the sight of the French tricolour—, Rammohun had rushed eagerly to the deck of his steamer to salute it as a symbol of patriotism. Vivekananda further admitted that he had already visited some Indian princes with a view to create a powerful organization to overthrow British rule from India. He had gone to the extent of negotiating with his friend—the gunmaker Sir Hiram Maxim to import fire-arms for this purpose.[4] He had informed Sakharam Ganesh Deuskar (1869-1912) that the entire country had become a storehouse of explosives and—*svalpamapyasya dharmasya*—even a tiny spark would set everything ablaze.[5] Romain Rolland rightly observed how that spark from Vivekananda's pyre—three years after his death—took hold of the subcontinent.[6] Did not the intense desire which Vivekananda had kindled in the people's mind for the political freedom of the country—in the name of the spiritual progress of humanity—flare into a conflagration under the charisma of Sri Aurobindo's leadership, on the foil of the Partition of Bengal in 1905?

Though Sri Aurobindo could have probably met Vivekananda between 1893 and 1899, while visiting his grandfather Rajnarain Basu (1826-99) at Deoghar, it is beyond surmise that the latter's torch was indeed passed on to him by Nivedita[7] when she met him at Baroda in 1902, soon after the Swami's cremation—that torch which was to be qualified as *devatar deep*

("The Lamp of God") by Rabindranath Tagore (1861-1941), in his famous "Salutation to Aurobindo". We have been informed that Nivedita had "read earlier with profound admiration" Sri Aurobindo's articles in the *Indu Prakash*, whereas it is evident that "Sri Aurobindo glimpsed in her the Shakti that had made her the inspired author of Kali, the Mother...In 1903 he appointed her a member of the controlling revolutionary committee of five..."[8]

We shall presently discover how the obvious and valuable link—as yet missing—between Vivekananda and Sri Aurobindo took place. It all began when in 1903, at the house of Yogendra Vidyabhushan (1845-1904), Sri Aurobindo met for the first time the as yet less known Jatindranath Mukherjee (1879-1915), to be very soon popular as Bagha Jatin. In him Sri Aurobindo was to recognize his "right-hand man", corroborated by several official and confidential reports of the colonial police.

Bhupendra Kumar Dutta

Brought up by Vinodebala Devi, Bagha Jatin's elder sister and alter ego, we listened to her tales of a glorious brother. Persuaded that the nation would one day like to know who he was, she left several written notes. In 1955, I started a serious research on the life and the times of Bagha Jatin, my grandfather. Exchanging letters with and meeting people who had known him prepared me considerably to move further in my investigation. At this juncture, Bhupendra Kumar Datta—one of the "barons" of the *Jugantar* and devoted to the memory of the departed leader—invited me, in 1963, to assist him in exploring documents at the State and National Archives—with a special permission from Jawaharlal Nehru, the then Prime Minister. I had access to the microfilms of the Indo-German Plot in Kaiserlich Deutsch, freshly received from the U.S. Archives. After a series of profuse revisions, in 1965, Datta encouraged me to serialize in the weekly *Basumati* of Kolkata my biography—*Sadhak Biplabi Jatindranath*. In a book-form publication of the West Bengal Book Board, it is running a second edition, congratulated by eminent historians and authors.

On reaching Paris in 1966 with a French government scholarship, while writing a first thesis at the old Sorbonne university—successfully defended in 1970—I consulted several archives, mainly in the UK. Since 1974, Raymond Aron accepted to supervise my thesis for the State Doctorate on the pre-Gandhian freedom movement in India (1893-1918)—on going through my documents, he qualified the project to be a "missing link in our history". Almost at the tail end of my enterprise, he suggested that a visit to the U.S. Archives would help me considerably. With his help, a Fulbright scholarship permitted to consult major archives, coast to coast. Several years after I defended it with distinction, the original thesis in French came out, with a foreword by Jacques Attali, calling it "a fascinating thesis".[9]

Raymond Aron

As yet unpublished in English, passages of this thesis inspired me to write the present book. There is a scope of writing three or four more similar books with the remaining chapters of the thesis. Invited by the Committee celebrating the 150th anniversary of Swami Vivekananda's birth, I had contributed one of these chapters to the symposium "Understanding Vivekananda", and I thank the Ramakrishna Mission Institute of Culture, Kolkata for their permission. I thank my French publisher M. Matthieu Boisdron. 2014 also marks the year that I have been awarded the prestigious Prix Hirayama by the members of the French Academy (*Inscriptions et Belles-Lettres*) during its session of 13 June 2014, for my recent publications in French: (1) *Les racines intellectuelles du mouvement d'independance de l'Inde* (1893-1918), Codex Publishers, 2010; (2) *Le Spontane: reflection on the Sahaja yana cult through Charya and Bâul Songs*, Almora Publishers, 2014; (3) *A Shade Sharp, a Shade Flat: trilingual anthology with introduction, notes and 108 poems by Rabindranath Tagore*, Shahitya Prakash, Dhaka, 2013.

I am grateful for the precious enthusiasm of my friend Dr. Prasenjit Sen and Ms Sonavi Desai of Indus Source Books.

~Dr. Prithwindra Mukherjee
Chevalier dans l'Ordre des Arts et des Lettres
Paris, 25 September 2014

CHAPTER I

SWAMI VIVEKANANDA
(1863-1902)

CHAPTER I

SWAMI VIVEKANANDA (1863-1902)

Introduction

Inspired by the teachings of the nineteenth century religious reformers, the highly qualified heir of a princely state was boasting to impress upon his guest—a distinguished monk—his great joy of having got rid of all forms of idol worship, considering himself to be, at last, a man liberated from superstitions. While admiring the picture gallery of the royal ancestors, the monk congratulated him for this achievement.

"Well, here is my grandfather, a famous hunter. And here is my father."

"Will you please take it down, O Maharaja?"

It was done. The monk asked the prince to spit on the portrait.

"I can't do it, Sir. This is my father."

"Are you joking? It is all mere paper covered with glass, lines in colour. How dare you worship this as your father?"

The monk was Swami Vivekananda, who thus revealed to

the prince a valuable secret of Indian tradition—loving and adoring a material object does not betray any polytheist belief. It merely proves that worshipping even a clay-made image is not necessarily prompted by any animist attachment; considering the image to be a symbol of God, one can realise the divine consciousness within by invoking it intently through the very material object chosen as a support. Earlier, though Maharshi Devendranath Tagore (1817-1905) had rejected several aspects of idolatry and initiated the Brahmo rites of marriage by replacing the *shalgram* stone, he had maintained the *homa* ritual around the sacred fire.

Genesis of a Renaissance

Both Rammohun Roy and Swami Dayanand (1824-83), in their zeal to reveal the secrets of a novel nationalism— out of the Vedanta and the Vedic texts respectively, had desired to rid the people's consciousness of a wild undergrowth that had cropped up: they both had looked down upon the cult of an embodied personal God as a number one public enemy. This attitude reached a degree of intolerance among their disciples belonging to the movements known as Brahmo and Arya Samaj. They seemed to take upon themselves to denounce all developments posterior to the Buddha's times (6th to 5th centuries B.C.), for the simple reason that they failed to bring up to date the justification of certain traditional values.

Swami Dayananad

Rabindranath Tagore

This was the epoch to be followed also by some other guiding lights, coming from the West. Maharshi's own son, Rabindranath, believed in the possibility of attaining God's proximity through Nature. As it is well known, since in Rabindranath's writings there are obvious traits of simultaneity with the thought of Schelling (1775-1854), much of all that the latter did was to exemplify the influence of Fichte (1762-1814) in his two-pronged quest: that of accepting Nature as the intermediary between man and God; and upholding art as the play-field of the Divine in the material world.

Quest for an Ideology

Another instance was Vivekananda, who stepped in with a further simultaneity: try to figure out the sense of the myths and the rites in their proper perspective (fantasizing instruments of the *puranas* helping people to grasp the lofty and abstract values of the Vedas and the Vedanta) and utilize common imagination in the process of sanctifying the apparently meaningless everyday life. We all know today that Swami Vivekananda is the monastic name of Narendranath Datta, a brilliant student in history and philosophy at the University of Calcutta. Like Rabindranath and other contemporaries, Vivekananda too, followed the example of Bankimchandra Chatterjee (1838-94), one of the first exponents in modern India, who revived the teachings of the *Bhagavad Gita* and of certain *puranas* and sequences from the epics (especially the *Mahabharata*). Vivekananda was to show how the vision of an ideal living cherished by the holy legends could endow human existence with a significance and serve the purpose of "man-making". In the doctrine of a universal good taught by Auguste Comte (1798-1857)—"disinterested care for the good of others" as interpreted, once again, by Bankimchandra—helped Vivekananda to come back to the starting point and explore the essence of the *Gita*, as we propose to examine. He discovered Comte's notion somewhat as a straightforward transposition of the spirit of altruism that the *Gita* professed: Vivekananda was to develop it further by reminding that the many is but manifestations of the One; service to the fellow creatures (*jiva*) is a service rendered to the Divine (*Shiva*). Pursuing his quest, he had looked for a synthesis also between the causality that he had learnt from Montesquieu (1689-1755), from the humanist dimension known through Fichte, and the love of liberty preached by Thomas Carlyle (1795-1881). Above all, Vivekananda maintained his admiration for mythologies that he had known since his childhood. He had studied French in order to appreciate the historic writings of his senior contemporary, Gaston Maspero (1846-1916).

National Navagopal

Vivekananda's athletic bearing was considerably helped by a training in the Indian arts of self-defence. His alert intelligence was endowed with a quick way of understanding and assimilating. He was a gifted singer of select classical music.[10] Son of the attorney Vishvanath Datta (1835-84), his childhood dream had been to replace his father's coachman—nobody knows whether it was out of the child's fascination for the powerful beast, or else, even more symptomatically, a sign of solidarity with the underprivileged creatures. While talking about another of his dreams that obsessed him later, young Narendra (future Vivekananda) admitted that he had been swayed between the desire of earning enormously and gaining immense power on one side and, on the other, leading an humble ascetic life of renunciation. Like other adolescents of his time, he participated—along with Bipinchandra Pal (1858-1932) and Rabindranath—in the demonstrations of physical culture within the framework of the National Fair (*Hindu Mela*) and was introduced to its organiser, Navagopal Mitra (1842-94), maliciously nicknamed *National* Navagopal. Personally appreciated by Devendranath, and by his guru Rajnarain Basu (1826-99), Navagopal had roused among the youth a puissant passion for everything national, a current of patriotic fervour. Students by hundreds, drawn by his enthusiasm, took the oath of serving the Motherland. Under the liberal governorship of George Campbell (1823-1900), while a compulsory course in gymnastics was introduced in the schools and colleges all over the country, as a counterpart, Navagopal supplied training in traditional arts of self-defence and even shooting. In his survey of history, Bankimchandra had come to sense that the people of Bengal had never been physically strong owing to four reasons: lack of initiative, of unity, of courage, and of perseverance. In order to mend this chronic deficiency, they required the determination to improve themselves. According to Bankimchandra, physical strength is not by itself an improvement, but a means to attain it. An unfulfilled determination leads to mental suffering which, at its climax, leads to disdain for comforts welling from apathy and indolence. Thus appears the spirit of enterprise. When, simultaneously, that determination gets hold of a collectivity, all enterprise reaches a unity. Courage emerges when that determination gets intense enough to be able to sacrifice one's life for a cause. An impetuous determination, by reaching stability, turns into perseverance.[11] Bankimchandra was convinced that by following this four-fold path of self-improvement (*anushilan*), Bengalis could achieve an extraordinary status.

Glory, O Motherland!

Rajnarain, in his autobiography, mentions how instinctively his friend Devendranath shunned the company of the English, owing to an inherent incompatibility between his opinions and theirs.[12] Rajnarain embodied a poignant patriotic yearning. Towards the end of his life, in 1898, Vivekananda was to go to Deoghar and spend a few days in the company of Rajnarain, who was proud of his grandson Aurobindo (poet and visionary), who had returned to India after fourteen years of studies in England. Bipinchandra on his side never forgot the warrior-like passion behind the white hair and white beard of Rajnarain, this thinker, who told him : "Naturally I do not expect to live longer. But before dying, if I can at least annihilate a single enemy of my country, I shall consider my life to be of worth."[13] Jyotirindra Tagore (1849-1925), another son of Devendranath and follower of Rajnarain, had set kindling the flame of a new valour and heroism in Young India by reviving the memory of ancient Indian values. Keeping in view the glorious image of patriotism as shown by Devendranath and Rajnarain, the leaders of the new generation—like Jyotirindra and Navagopal—believed that physical strength was indispensable for driving the English out of India. In a flash of economists' intuition they felt the urgency of recovering the entire management of trade and commerce from the hands of the English. They decided to discard foreign products from Indian markets. They looked forward to encouraging and improving native agriculture and industry.

Bhupendranath Datta

During those years of national awakening, according to Bhupendranath Datta (Narendra's younger brother, himself a revolutionary), Surendranath Banerjee and Anandamohan Basu through their Students' Association had a great appeal to the youth in favour of an intensive physical training and a militant attitude against the oppressor. Narendra had thoroughly studied works of Bankimchandra. Keeping the latter's programme of self-education (*anushilan*), he had been trained in traditional wrestling and self-defence at the gymnasium of Ambu Guha (1843-1900). In his family library there were also volumes of the fiery writings of Yogendra Vidyabhushan (1845-1904). Narendra, Abindranath, Bipinchandra—three stalwarts of the generation—derived lessons from the experience of the *Hindu Mela* in how to excel in contests and demonstrations of physical education; they learnt how an orator through his speech or a musician through his compositions could earn the praise of the public for their urge to serve the country. Navagopal and Naren were cousins.[14] As soon as Dr. Mahendra Nandi manufactured a novel handloom and wove the first samples of his coarse towels, his friend Jyotirindra, with the gait of a proud prince, wore it like a turban and danced all over the market; shortly after, Rabindranath composed his famous song,

> *Adorn your head with the coarse cloth that the*
> *Mother has given!*

Accompanied by Dr. Nandi and others, Jyotirindra was seen going to the southern outskirts of Calcutta apparently for hunting birds; in reality, they prepared young militants by teaching them the use of firearms. We have heard how stern Rabindranath's voice could be: "Must we then go and agitate before the English! In utter humility we make way for the English; in the administrations we assume the insult and hatred of the English boss; we go to their home to call them our father and our mother to seek favour from them; we salute their cooks and grooms and please them by calling *Khan Sahib* and *Chacha*; finding us seated on benches inside a public park, the English rush to get hold of our neck to drive us off; the English bar our access to their clubs; inside trains, the English reserve their own separate seats; by *gentleman*, the English designate the English only and by *Baboo*, they mean the chicken-hearted clerical slaves. The English do not consider our life to be more precious than the life of the animals they eat. The English come to our homes to teach us lessons. We cannot protest. Are we now about to agitate before the English: give us rights equal to yours!...Will the fact of donning a constitutional lion's skin make claws jut in place of hooves!...Those who cannot hold their own prestige high, what the hell others have to care for coming to bestow honour on us?"[15]

At this juncture, expecting Narendra Datta to shine as a jurist after his higher studies in England, his father Vishvanath had enrolled him as an apprentice to the firm of his colleague, the attorney, Nimaichandra Basu. Since it was quite laudable among upper class Indians of the time to become members of Free Mason Lodge, Vishvanath encouraged Narendra to join this select club of the privileged.[16] But destiny had decided otherwise, with the sudden death of Vishvanath.

Have you seen God?

At the age of about twenty, mad-like, Vivekananda had been running to spiritual guides one after the other, asking point blank: "Have you seen God?" Born in a Brahmo family, disappointed by the fact that the Religion of Humanity professed by Comte could not help him solve the problem of the Evil in Nature and in man's nature, he returned to Brahmoism in search for an answer. Rather displeased with the theosophical and intuitionist counsel from Devendranath (who had been Rammohun's spiritual heir), Vivekananda went to Dakshineshwar to meet an obscure priest at the temple of Kali. The person, Sri Ramakrishna (1836-1886), affirmed candidly on listening to his query: "Of course I see God, as concretely as I see you." At the end of six long years of tussle between Reason and Revelation, Vivekananda yielded to the inner riches of the Seer—"who puts into practice whatever he says and who has surrendered everything for the benefit of God"—in order to be the spokesman of God. "His very life itself," wrote Vivekananda, "helped me understand what the Scriptures signify."[17] After Sri Ramakrishna's passing, Vivekananda, with a handful of fellow disciples, founded a new order—Sri Ramakrishna Mission—to live the teachings of the Master who affirmed that *jiva* (the created being) is but a form of Shiva (the Supreme Being). During seven long years, as a wandering monk, he visited India thoroughly in order to identify himself with the aspirations of his motherland and of his countrymen, in order to determine the possible role of spirituality in a future resurgent India.

The Pragmatic Saint

Storming the doors of the Parliament of the World's Religions at Chicago, in 1893, Vivekananda wrested an immediate fame thanks to his proclaiming a creed in the name of Vedanta, one of the most ancient spiritual traditions of humanity, that which had been revived by Sri Ramakrishna. The monks of his faith learnt how to comfort social ills of humanity, somewhat in the manner that Comte had done (with an essential difference of vision—replacing God by society). Vivekananda knew it for certain that India's political freedom was indispensable for the spiritual progress of humanity. Furious with the misery and the hunger that weighed on India, Vivekananda was to roar:

> "Bread! Bread! I do not believe in a God who is unable to give some bread! I do not believe in a God who cannot give me bread here, giving me eternal bliss in heaven! Pooh, India is to be raised, the poor are to be fed, education is to be spread, and the evil of priest-craft is to be removed. No priest-craft, no social tyranny! More bread, more opportunity for everybody! Our young fools make meetings to get more power from the English. They only laugh. None deserves liberty who is not ready to give liberty. Suppose the English give over to you all the power. Why, the powers that be then, will hold the people down, and let them not have it. Slaves want power to make slaves."[18]

Vivekananda had in mind the attitude of Indian society which always considered an individual to be its slave, whereas India's religious thinking has been exemplarily liberal. According to him, in the West just the opposite has contributed a less tyrannical society and a more intolerant religion. His ardent wish was to see Indian society make a greater effort in remedying the misery of its people and care less for the spiritual deliverance of an elite.

Thus, thanks to Vivekananda's initiative, the religion of Vedanta was turning into a regenerative driving force for the entire national, social, economic and above all political life. It warned the people of the West against their excess of dynamism (*rajas*), and Indians against their excessive inertia (*tamas*).[19] Looking down on the reform bills proposed by the contemporary political leaders, he put forward his own scheme of constructions by moulding the personality of each individual Indian, by promoting each one of them to the status of a personal dignity. Be he a peasant, a menial worker, a cobbler or even a garbage collector, he wanted them all to have education.[20] Analyzing the reasons behind the national inertia, Vivekananda advised: "First educate the nation, create your legislative body, and then the law will be forthcoming. First create the power, the sanction from which the law will spring. The kings are gone; where is the new sanction, the new power of the people? Bring it up. Therefore, even for social reform, the first duty is to educate the people, and you will have to wait till that time comes."[21] Vivekananda meant by education: "The training, by which the current and expression of will are brought under control and become fruitful, is called education."[22]

The Educationist

Foreseeing the need of a national system of education which would be managed by Indians themselves, Vivekananda prophesied: "The education that you are getting now has some good points, but it has a tremendous disadvantage which is so great that the good things are all weighed down. In the first place it is not a man-making education, it is merely and entirely a negative education...Any training based on negation, is worse than death... And the result is, that fifty years of such education has not produced one original man...Every man of originality that has been produced has been educated elsewhere, and not in this country, or they have gone to the old universities once more to cleanse themselves of superstitions. Education is not the amount of information that is put into your brain and runs riot there, undigested, all your life. We must have life-building, man-making, character-making assimilation of ideas. If you have assimilated five ideas and made them your life and character, you have more education than any man who has got by heart a whole library."[23]

About a score of years before the Russian revolution, while Vivekananda was busy determining the profit India could make out of materialism, he analyzed the nature of a capitalist society: "The material tyranny is tremendous. The wealth and power of a country are in the hands of a few men who do not work, but manipulate the work of millions of human beings. By this power they can deluge the whole earth with blood. Religion and all things are under their feet; they rule and stand supreme. The Western world is governed by a handful of Shylocks. All those things that you hear about—constitutional government, freedom, liberty and parliaments—are but jokes. The West is groaning under the tyranny of Shylocks, and the East is groaning under the tyranny of the Priests: each must keep the other in check."[24] Here, Vivekananda does not raise any racist question by mentioning Shylock; in his Bengali essay "East and West" he has compared the food habits of the Jews and the Hindus. Here the object of his banter are the Vaishyas–the way they govern the world by sheer commercial knack and power is similar to that of the *kshatriyas* who rule by usurping the control of the *brahmans*. In a Bengali essay he wrote: "Those who possess capital, hold the rein of the government in their hands, plunder and suck the blood of their subjects, send them to die as sepoys in the four corners of the world; victorious, they will grow richer with properties and cereals, whereas their subjects will die on the spot."[26]

Champion of the Oppressed

Vivekananda qualified the tremendous potential force of the Indian proletariat as the "Sleeping Leviathan" and he questioned his young disciples: "What will you do with your personal deliverance (*mukti*)? The very desire for such a deliverance is extremely selfish. Enough of meditation, enough of deliverance. Go where people are struck by epidemics, where they are groaning, where they are dying of famine. At the most you will get killed. Worms like you and me are born and are dying constantly. In which way can that modify the world? Go and die for a noble cause. Since die we must, why not die for a noble cause?"[26] An echo of this message is reiterated in his "Conversations and Dialogues": "I will rouse them through the infallible power of Vedic mantras. I am born to proclaim to them that fearless message: 'Arise! Awake!' Be you my helpers in this work. Go over from village to village, from one portion of the country to another, and preach this lesson of fearlessness to all, from the *brahman* to the *chandal*.[27] Tell each and all that infinite power resides within them, that they are sharers of Immortal Bliss... First make the people of the country stand on their legs by rousing their inner power, first let them learn to have good food and clothes and plenty of enjoyment—then tell them how to be free from this bondage of enjoyment."[28]

In "My Plan of Campaign", Vivekananda declared without hesitation: "I believe in patriotism, and I have also my own ideal of patriotism. Do you feel? Do you feel that millions and millions of the descendants of gods and of sages have become next-door neighbours to brutes? Do you feel that millions are starving today, and millions have been starving for ages? Do you think that ignorance has come over the land as a dark cloud? Does it make you restless? Does it make you sleepless? Has it gone into your blood, coursing through your veins, becoming consonant with your heart-beats? Has it made you almost mad? Are you seized with that one idea of the misery of ruin, and have you forgotten all about your name, your fame, your wives, your children, your property, even your own bodies? Have you done that? That is the first step to become a patriot, the very first step."[29]

In a lecture at Madras, on 14 February 1897, Vivekananda openly invited his listeners to accept for a period of fifty years the Motherland—"this Supreme Mother"—as the only object of worship, forgetting about the other inefficient divinities: "All the divinities are asleep, except the only one who is looking after your national life; her hand is everywhere, everywhere her ears, she is omnipresent." Apropos of the message of a masterpiece of India's traditional wisdom—the *Mahanirvana Tantra*—Vivekananda enumerated the duties of an ideal citizen: "The family head has to be a hero as far as his enemies are concerned. He has to resist them, that is his duty. He has not to sit in a corner for lamenting and narrating rubbish in favour of his non-resistance. If he does not behave heroically with his enemies, he fails in his duty. And for his friends and his relatives, he has to be as meek as a lamb. The family head has the duty of not showing respect to the wicked ones, because if he appears to be deferential before them, he encourages them in their wickedness. He commits a serious mistake if he disdains those who deserve respect, the ones who are right. His friendship has to be controlled, he must not look for new friends everywhere; he must observe the actions of those to whom he wants to extend friendship, watch how they behave with others, think over it and, then only, accept them as friends."[30]

Aware of the hostility of the *brahman* orthodoxy towards Rammohun's very first attempt to translate sacred Sanskrit texts into Bengali and English, Vivekananda found the medieval monopoly of the priests rather satanic. They held that if an untouchable (*shudra*) listened to the Vedic chant, he would deserve to have his ears sealed with molten lead: if he further uttered a single verse from it, his tongue was to be chopped off. Recognizing that "such devils sometimes arose among the ancients," Vivekananda noted how, down the centuries, the *brahmans* grew more tolerant in accepting that the *shudras* could as well imitate the brahmans.[31] He had no sympathy for caste arrogance, admitting the essential quality of all men: "I can perform one duty in social life, and you another; you can govern a country and I can mend a pair of old shoes, but that is no reason why you are greater than I; for can you mend my shoes?"[32]

Vivekananda believed that the fact of belonging to a caste was no matter of birth, but the free choice of the individual. Everybody, according to his temperament and his vocation, chooses his appurtenance to the corporate rank (*jati*) of teachers and scholars (*brahman*), of warriors (*kshatriya*), of businessmen and industrialists (*vaishya*), and other liberal professions (*shudra*). From this point of view, Vivekananda stood by the side of the illustrious demystifiers like Rammohun, Vidyasagar and Ranade. In *A Plan of Work for India*, he reminded: "The present caste is not the real *jati*, but a hindrance to its progress. It really has prevented the free action of *jati*, i.e. caste or variation...Whenever any nation ceases to produce this immense variety, it must die...India fell because you prevented and abolished caste. Every frozen aristocracy or privileged class is a blow to caste and is not caste. Let *jati* have its sway, break down every barrier in the way of caste, and we shall rise."[33] Even if the caste system had divided the people, Vivekananda held that it has also united them, because all the members of the caste were bound to help their fellows in times of need. He also believed that thanks to a gradual perfection, each being could finally attain the supreme status of a Brahman. Merciless in front of all doctrine and all practice of untouchability, Vivekananda meant to put a drastic end to such abuses which arose out of a misunderstanding of true Indian tradition. Sharing this view with him, Rabindranath Tagore wrote several poems in 1910, that could be considered as their joint manifesto:

Unfortunate, O my Motherland: all those whom you have humiliated,
You must feel equal to them in their humiliation.
Those whom you have denied the simple rights of a man,
Those whom you kept waiting without taking them in your arms,
You must feel equal to them in their humiliation.
Day by day, having dismissed the contact of these people,
You have scorned the God that indwells their heart.
Those whom you shove downwards will thrust you farther down,
Those whom you want to surpass keep on dragging you still behind.[34]

National Consciousness

Asked about the efficient means to shake the national consciousness, Vivekananda replied to the agent of the *Madras Times,* in February 1897 that the greatest national sin was to neglect the proletariat, which he took to be one of the reasons of India's downfall; he insisted that no amount of politics would be of any use as long as the masses of the country did not receive proper education, sufficient food and adequate healthcare. It is they who paid for our education, who built our temples, only to receive in return kicks. They were literally our slaves. If we wanted India to stand up, we would have to work for her. Vivekananda spoke about his wish to launch two central institutions: one, first of all, in Madras, and the other in Calcutta, for training young missionaries. He placed his confidence in the young generation, in the modern generation out of which emerged his disciples. Like lions, they were to pounce upon the problems. Vivekananda claimed to have formulated the idea and to have spent his life with this end in view. If he did not succeed, someone better would take his cue for its execution, and Vivekananda would be happy to fight for it. The only question that mattered was that of giving the masses their rights. India owns the noblest of the religions ever known in the world, whereas Indians keep on feeding their proletariat on nothing at all.[35] The proletariat among us is sunk in ignorance and overwhelmed with distress! Sri Aurobindo had exclaimed on returning to India in 1893.[36] Throughout his life, Vivekananda persistently fought against the sad system of castes and, therefore, against untouchability. Agreeing with Vilfredo Pareto (1848-123) who, too, was a champion of social mobility, Vivekananda believed in "the mobility of the elites." He even foresaw a reign of the *shudras*, those who—down the centuries—have been trampled, crushed and exploited as the lower classes: endowed with the economic perspicacity of the Vaishyas (businessmen), with the force and the valour of the *kshatriyas* (warriors) and the spiritual energy of the *brahmans* (possessing wisdom), they were to assume the new face of Aryan culture: "The first glow of this power has already begun to slowly break upon the Western world, and the thoughtful are at their wits' end to reflect upon the final issue of this fresh phenomenon. Socialism, Anarchism, Nihilism and other like sects are the vanguard of the social revolution that is to follow."[37]

Literally persuaded by the confirmations of the Sacred Texts, he made a gift of the syllable AUM to his disciples—irrespective of their appurtenance (*shudra*, Muslim, Christians from Europe and America)—welcomed them all, without any exception, as *brahmans*. He was persuaded that it is not a son of a *brahman* who becomes *brahman* owing to his birth. And this attitude of Vivekananda's has been amply approved by Indian tradition. The castes (*varna*), according to him, have been ascending landings or successive spring-boards towards the supreme status of a hierarchical society. While speaking of this hierarchy, Nivedita was to find an analogy between the system of castes and the honours bestowed by the British Crown; she was to appreciate each caste to be a promotion leading towards the supreme distinction.

Whereas the lives and works of Dayananda, Bankimchandra or Tilak have been—often unjustly—interpreted as reactionary voices to claim the Hindu supremacy (at the cost of and ruling out the Indian Muslims), those of Vivekananda remain beyond all such ambiguity and concession. On the basis of his personal knowledge of Muslim doctrine and the experiences of Islam of his master (Sri Ramakrishna) underwent, Vivekananda could uphold that—for the common man—the Vedantic theories would become obsolete and futile as long as they do not receive the pragmatic support of Islam. On 10 June 1898, he wrote in a letter to a Muslim admirer that the non-dualism as it has been structured in India was to suit the purpose of the entire mankind of the future: for so doing, with a view to attain a universality and to look upon the entire human race as one's own soul, much has yet to be done. "For our own motherland a junction of the two great systems, Hinduism and Islam—Vedanta brain and Islam body—is the only hope. I see in my mind's eye the future perfect India rising out of this chaos and strife..."[38] In the same letter, Vivekananda cast a farther glance with the hope to "lead mankind to the place where there is neither the Vedas, nor the Bible, nor the Koran; yet this has to be done by harmonizing the Vedas, the Bible and the Koran. Mankind ought to be taught to learn that religions are but the varied expressions of the Religion, which is Oneness, so that each may choose the path that suits him best." He was to assure further: "A Christian does not have to be converted Hindu or Buddhist, neither a Hindu or a Buddhist converted Christian. Each one has to assimilate the spirit of the others, keeping one's individuality intact."[39]

He who kindled in his young disciples, the ardent will to get rid of all bonds of slavery—including, and above all, political bondage—did not hesitate to fashion his internationalist vision specifying that his interests extended to all the nations far beyond India alone. He was heard challenging that he was born not to live and die like those cowards collapsing under castes, superstitious, merciless, hypocrite, atheist that is so common among the Hindus of the educated classes. He belonged to India as much as to the rest of the world: "Which country dares claim its exclusive right on me? Am I servant of any single people?"

CHAPTER II

NIVEDITA
(1867-1911)

CHAPTER II

NIVEDITA (1867-1911)

Introduction

Margaret Noble, Vivekananda's spiritual daughter, was better known as Nivedita ("The Dedicated"). Before she was introduced to the Master in London in 1895, she had been strongly drawn towards novel experiments in teaching, especially towards the methods of Pestalozzi and Froeble. With her degree from the Halifax College, having taught for over eight years, Nivedita had opened her *Ruskin School* in 1892 at Wimbledon. Inquisitive by spirit, she collaborated with several avant-garde movements such as *Free Ireland*, the new socialism, anarchism as professed by Prince Kropotkine (1842-1921) whom she had known personally. In her seeking for the truth, Nivedita came across Vivekananda, accepted him as Master, before settling in India in January 1898.

Taken over by the face of cruelty and hypocrisy assumed by British politics in India, she discovered in Vivekananda's personality the champion of the movement for the political freedom of the country which she adopted as her own.

Sanguine about the obstructive role of British imperialism in the evolution of a glorious nation doomed to guiding humanity towards its spiritual fulfillment, Nivedita with her body and soul participated in the renaissance of India. Sensitive to Vivekananda's indignation against India's political and economic slavery, to his emotion aroused by every echo of humiliation suffered by his countrymen, admiring his enthusiasm to infuse a fresh virility in the national character, Nivedita readily welcomed his spiritual yearnings in perfect fusion with the militant aspirations of India to win her unconditional freedom. In her eyes Vivekananda appeared to be the oracle of Kali, the dreadful Mother, destroyer of Evil. He taught her to adore in Kali, the terrible Mother, to offer herself to death. Death that was not to be the suicide of a coward or a weakling: he encouraged to woo death as does a heroic soul who knows that, after all, there is no other solution than dying. Vivekananda repeated that he loved the terrible because it is terrible, desperation because it is desperate, misery because it is misery. He urged her to keep on fighting, recognising the momentary defeat as the very condition of that fight. That was his ideal: "the only ideal". Having blessed Nivedita for her resolution to pursue this heroic path, Vivekananda had assured her that by following that earthly mission, if she were but his creation she would at the most get destroyed; but she would be immortal if she had been created by the Mother herself.

Field Work

During a recurrence of epidemic, in 1898, Jatindranath Mukherjee, with his friends—already engaged in social relief—joined Nivedita, defying the formal ban against cremating victims of cholera and plague, as much as the untouchables. She wrote of Jatindra: "A young man came to see me, who aspires to raise the youth of India in the name of the Swami. Full of admiration for the Master, himself, he is all strength. He is independent and, over all, a Brahman!"[40] She further wrote in a London newspaper: "A religious order, unique in its kind, uniting Christians, Muslims and Hindus, has created a phenomenon of charity without equal since the

Buddha's times. Ten thousand human beings have been saved of famine in a single month."[41] When Nivedita wanted to inform Vivekananda about Jatindra, she discovered that they already had known each other.

On 26 April 1899, Nivedita wrote to her Norwegian friend, Ole Bull: "I hate my compatriots, knowing them to be so mean...Alas, the glorious days for the English are not yet over in India. I shall await it with all my heart. I pray to be reborn in order to win back for India the dear liberty and cry out, 'Long live young India!', just as had roared the young revolutionaries by Mazzini's side, to liberate Italy!"[42] Having known through Surendra Tagore the impatience of Jatindra's group to be politically active, she encouraged Surendra, in 1900, to invite Jatindra and his associate Bhavabhushan to a meeting of the founders of the Anushilan: in his enthusiasm, Jatindra was to open several branches of the Anushilan in Kushtia and several neighbouring towns in Nadia and Jessore.[43] In 1902, after Swamiji's demise, while visiting Baroda, in Sri Aurobindo Nivedita detected the revolutionary leader that Vivekananda would have liked to guide: when she told him that Bengal was waiting for him, probably she kept in mind the patriotic substructure Jatindra had been fast creating. She wrote to her American friend Josephine Macleod: "Whereas India was absorbed in her quest for knowledge, a hoard of brigands had pounced on her. It is up to India now to take back the possession of her field after having driven the brigands off. As soon as India will decide to look after defending herself, she can utilize every element foreign to it."[44]

Mother of the Indian People

Faithful to her comprehension of the Swami's message, Nivedita wrote that arts, sciences and religions are but three different ways of expressing the same truth. For this very reason, she remained available to Indian scientists like Jagadish Chandra Bose and Prafulla Chandra Ray. She was to encourage the artistic blossoming of the founders of the Calcutta School of Arts such as Abanindra Tagore and Nandalal Basu (in spite of his sympathy for the Extremist wing of freedom fighters). She maintained the friendliest of relationships with the All-India leaders, both Moderates and the Radicals, with the hope of rapidly cementing the nascent nationalist consciousness under the unifying eyes of Vivekananda. In an obituary published in the November 1911 issue of the *Pravasi*, Rabindranath singled out Nivedita as the "mother of the Indian people" endowed with a multidimensional genius and an inner sight. The veteran leader Surendranath Banerjee was to write that Nivedita had installed at the heart of all her action, all her thought and all the beats of her life, hope and ideal for India. He sensed that the liberated soul of one of the prophets of yore had taken birth in that body, to serve her people. Each sentence of her writings betrays a rare capacity of assimilating and containing the Indian spirit.[45]

Author of a sociological survey of India, *Web of Indian Life,* Nivedita drew the admiration of several Western sociologists like Patrick Geddes, F.R. Alexander, S.K. Ratcliffe, S.H. Swiny. Her influence had directly guided certain future celebrities like Surendranath Tagore, Dinesh Chandra Sen, Sir Jadunath Sarkar, Bhupendranath Datta and O.C. Ganguli.

Radical Politics

When on 6 January 1902, Kakuzo Okakura (1862-1913), a Japanese historian of art, came to Calcutta to meet Vivekananda and request him to preside over the forthcoming international Parliament of the World's Religions, the Swami declined the invitation. Nobody as yet knew that he had only seven months of life before him. Urged by Okakura to be introduced to the Indian revolutionary elements and to organise a movement of Pan-Asiatic solidarity to overthrow European domination, Vivekananda directed Nivedita to take him to the "Ballyganj boys". Not too endearing, this term designated Rabindranath and the coterie of his frivolous admirers. Invited by Surendra Tagore (1872-1940), when Jatindra met Okakura, much amused by the former's excellent English, Okakura muttered: "I hope no Japanese will learn to speak English so well!"

Somewhat induced by the Japanese playboy, Nivedita agreed to rewrite his manuscript and add a foreword for *The Ideals of the East*, which Okakura was to get published from London in 1904. Diffident of Okakura's integrity, Vivekananda warned Nivedita against his subversive activities. Having known the Swami's liking for an armed revolution against the imperial tyranny (to the extent of approaching the gun-maker Hiram Maxim for importing for this purpose firearms with ammunition), Nivedita could not very well understand her Master's refusal to collaborate with the Japanese. In an interview, in 1937, Ratcliffe—Nivedita's journalist friend—was to tell Jean Herbert how prompt Nivedita had been in sensing the Swami's intuitive reticence concerning Okakura. The latter's mission in India was that of a political espionage, quite in keeping with the Japanese attack of Korea. On 1 May 1908, Nivedita was to write: "Had I a better understanding of the real significance of the book (*The Ideals of the East)*, I would have never extended any collaboration."[46]

Vivekananda seems to have told Tilak how helplessly India depended on a foreign government—India's politics needed to have her inner sources, though her method was to be that of a struggle and of a self-defence. "Let it take a sufficiently important turn to get at last accepted by the government, all the demands of the people."[47] Simultaneously, Vivekananda insisted on having a secret formation of volunteers dedicated to the cause of the Motherland; it had to aim at creating a mentality in favour of a possible armed rising against British imperialism.

CHAPTER III

SRI AUROBINDO (1872-1950)

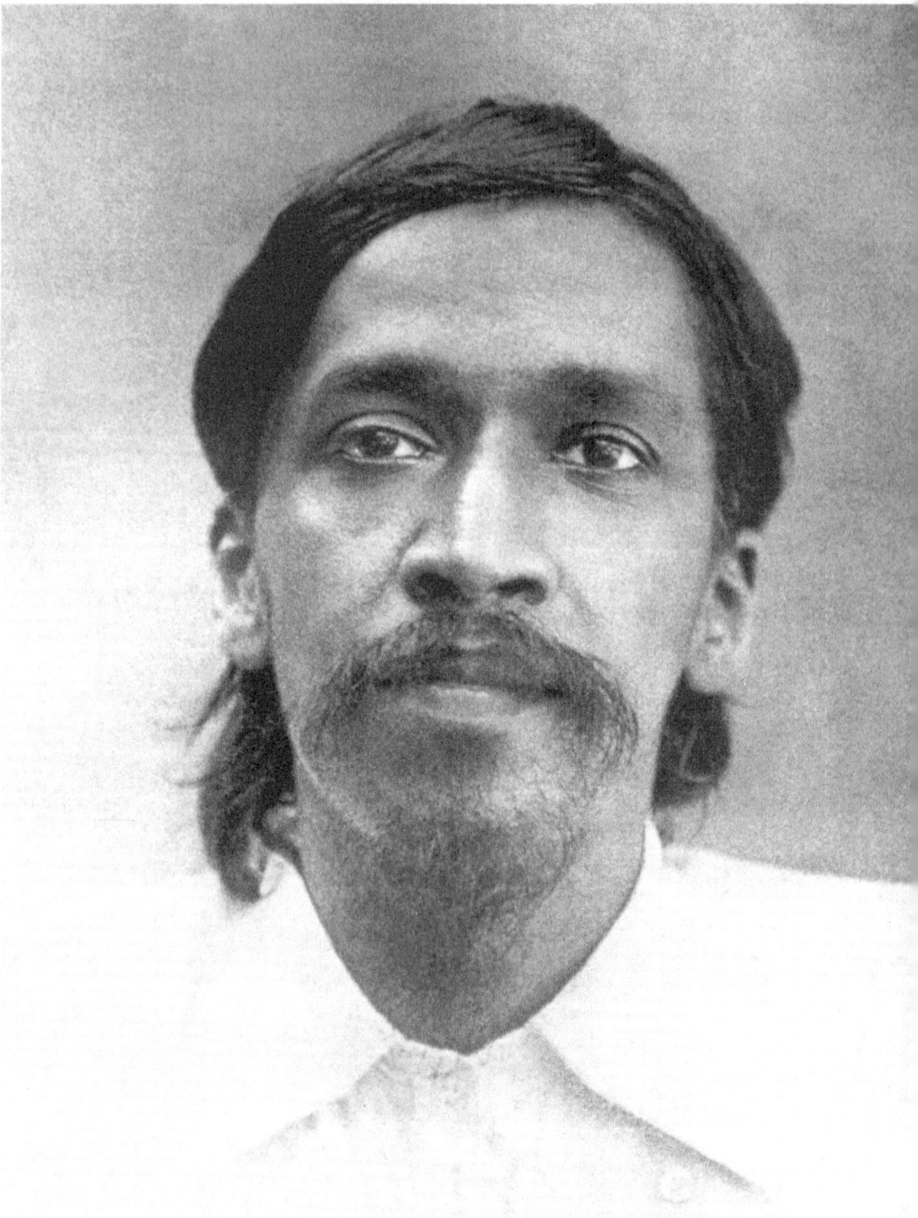

CHAPTER III

SRI AUROBINDO (1872-1950)

Introduction

Sri Aurobindo,[48] the third son of surgeon Krishnadhan Ghose (1846-93), was a privileged spiritual heir of Rammohun Roy, thanks to a direct transmission by his maternal grandfather, Rajnarain Basu. After two years spent in acquiring the degree of M.D. from Aberdeen University, Dr. Ghose had returned from England in 1871, convinced about the beneficent role of British culture in India. His extreme Anglicization will deprive Sri Aurobindo, since his birth, of all contact with native life and with Bengali, his mother tongue. After two years of primary studies in a strict English Convent school in Darjeeling, Sri Aurobindo, with his two elder brothers, went to Manchester in 1879 and did not return to India before 1893. Living with the family of the reverend William Drewett, a Latinist—, Aurobindo benefited from an intensive tutoring, practised English "better than an English boy of his age"[49] (a language in which he will compose and publish verses since his adolescence), would receive exceptional distinctions: first at St. Paul's School of London (1885-1890), then at King's College of Cambridge (1890-1892), for his excellence in Greek. He would devour classical and contemporary literatures, adding to it original masterpieces in French, Italian, Spanish and German. In spite of his initial interdiction, Dr. Ghose had started sending Aurobindo cuttings from Anglo-Indian press describing the miserable conditions of India under colonial rule. At this juncture, in Cambridge, Aurobindo read Mazzini and adhered to the activities of an association of Indian students, *Lotus and the Dagger*—vowed to the independence of India. After a First Class tripos in 1892, turning away from his administrative career in India—a cherished wish of his father—Aurobindo did not report for the riding test, in spite of his over-all success in the contest for admission.

Life at Baroda

Taking his service in the principality of Baroda in Gujarat, Aurobindo went back to India in February 1893, and began having a series of strange experiences with the descent of a "great calm".[50] Till then indifferent to all theistic preoccupations, he refused even to practise any Yoga postures, because he believed that a Yoga that required abandoning of the world did not interest him. His objective was to free the Motherland. Then, determined to seize the implications of his experiences, he agreed to try the path of the quest for the Absolute as taught by Indian tradition: he took it up seriously only when he had learned that the *tapasya* (asceticism) that one uses to escape the world could as well serve a life of action. He learned that through Yoga one could receive powers and persuaded himself: why the devil should he not acquire these powers for the liberation of the Motherland! Later, to the question, "So, in a very skilful way, God exploited your desire to free India?", Sri Aurobindo replied that it was first of all the moment for the Motherland, then came humanity and the rest nowhere. In his heart of hearts, something got the sanction of the intellect; he entered the spiritual life by a side door. Therefore, far from being incompatible with his activities of political insurrection, Aurobindo's spiritual effort, turned inward, will provide him with a superior vision and energy, making him the principal leader of the nationalist movement. He recalled having paid a visit to the great saint, Brahmananda of Chandod, and having been initiated to the cult of Kali (the divine Energy destructive of Evil)—at the end of a Vedic ceremony around the ritual fire, officiated by an accredited priest—intended for his success in the political mission. Later, in 1907, Aurobindo received from Lele Maharaj, the Marathi yogi, some concrete indications leading to an accelerated progress.

In Baroda, during twelve years, along with a surprising literary output, Sri Aurobindo established a programme of national emancipation. By turns, occupying administrative and educational responsibilities (Professor of English and French, then Rector of the State College), he sailed upstream towards the source of Indian civilisation. In addition to possessing Bengali (to the extent of using it for editorials published in his Bengali magazine, *Dharma*, in 1909), and learning some other major Indian languages (Hindi, Gujarati, Marathi and, later, Tamil), Aurobindo mastered Sanskrit and the Vedic texts, capable of exploring the mysteries of these old writings, of translating and commenting in English—with a new interpretation, in keeping with the initial objective of the seers of antiquity—the Vedas, the Upanishads, the Gita and of other fundamental texts including mythology and the epics. Up to then, these *new* significances escaped the grasp of the routine philologists. Sri Aurobindo affirmed, in his treatise on the philosophy of the Upanishads that, thanks to a number of inner disciplines and observances, the seers of ancient India had discovered—in their effort to surpass the limits of the physical, vital and mental instrument—some essential truths of the universe inside and outside themselves.

Deshpande, his friend of the Cambridge association, appointed editor of the magazine *Indu Prakash* of Bombay, offered Aurobindo a regular column, where he published during the years 1893-94 a series of nine political articles, *New*

Lamps for Old—an analysis that suggested drastic measures against the servility of the Moderate leaders of the National Congress. Exasperated by their policy "of flattery, prayers and petitions" with regard to the British government, Aurobindo qualified their timidity as "awful", their mind far from being "sincere and serious". "We are at present the blind if not led by the blind, at any rate by the one-eyed," he wrote about the bad choice of leaders and about their methods. Mentioning the example of the revolution in France (a country that—according to him—played the same role in the contemporary world as did Athens in ancient times), he observed that it was not an assembly of respectable citizens, but the vast ignorant proletariat that emerged out of a prolonged apathy, to erase in five terrifying years the tyranny accumulated during thirteen centuries. And Aurobindo underlined the imperious necessity to wake up, to enlighten and to drag the mass because, he found, the proletariat was the real key to the situation. Slumbering, it was; immobile, too; it did not represent any present strength, but it was an immense potential strength; anyone who managed to catch hold of this evidence and released this power became automatically the master of the future.

Simultaneously, for the first time since the arrival of the British in India, Sri Aurobindo gave vent to a pitiless but realist criticism of the colonial government and demystified before the Indians the divine superiority of the British, by a historic analysis of the systems of education, administration, society and politics of the European countries. The demystification became more concrete when Aurobindo ridiculed the loyalty of the Moderates towards Victoria calling her "Our Mother": he did not mince his words while recalling that the Queen-Empress was an old obese woman, about whom few citizens could really know or care anything. Or, when he denounced these English who governed India as men of an extreme triviality, but enjoying a privileged position—types of the middle bourgeois or the Philistine, to mention the lapidary English expression, with a narrow heart and mercantile habits quite fit for this sort of people.

Approached by Ranade, the moderate patriarch and spokesman of the Congress, Sri Aurobindo put an end to these exploding articles and undertook a few detailed essays on Bankimchandra Chatterjee who had just left this world: Sri Aurobindo declared him to be the visionary of a spiritualized patriotism.

The educational doctrine of the Vedic time, resuscitated by Dayananda's experiment, had drawn Sri Aurobindo's attention. In company of Deshpande, he founded a school, the Bharati Vidyalaya, in Ganganath, near the Narmada: in addition to usual disciplines, they introduced training in self-defence and in spirituality, under the guidance of Keshavananda, a monk who shared with Sri Aurobindo plans of political autonomy for India.

Since his arrival in Baroda, thanks to his political opinions and to his deep influence on the student circles, Sri Aurobindo was contacted by clandestine revolutionary cells that intended to launch a general movement throughout India. On meeting a certain Thakur Saheb of aristocratic origin hailing from the royal State of Udaipur and in charge of its branch in Maharashtra, Sri Aurobindo set off on a trip to Central India to negotiate his programme of uprising with Indian officers of a barrack of the British army; as President of the organisation in Gujarat, Sri Aurobindo was also fortunate to collaborate with B.G. Tilak. Often, during vacations, he visited his grandfather, Rajnarain Basu, at Deoghar, and enjoyed his enlightening presence and conversations.

Revolutionary Plans

Sri Aurobindo's revolutionary plans to form a generation of young militants dedicated to the cause of the Motherland—reinforced by Bankim's vision and by the cult of the divine Energy (Bhavaani, the goddess personalised by Shivaji)—very soon took the shape of the manifesto, the *Bhavaani Mandir*, to erect a "temple in honour of the Divine Mother". It was published from Baroda in 1904, simultaneously in English, Hindi and Bengali. The publication had for objective to found a community around a temple, situated in the forest at a summit close to Amarkantaka in Central India. The community's mission would be to execute the divine command of creating a nation, to Aryanise the world. "The nation is yours; the epoch is yours (…); the world is not a fragment of earth surrounded by ocean and hills, but the whole earth with her millions of souls." Aryanising in the context meant the re-establishing of values recognised as the most sacred in all traditions, in the name of the future of humanity. In a word, the point where converge action, love and knowledge.

After having trained a young Bengali patriot—Jatindra Banerjee who later became a monk known as Swami Niralamba—in the army of Baroda, Sri Aurobindo sent him to Bengal to work as his emissary. Thanks to letters of introduction that Sri Aurobindo handed him, Banerjee was welcomed by a number of powerful thinkers in Bengal, such as Barrister Pramatha Mitra (friend of Surendranath Banerjee), Sarala Devi (niece of Poet Tagore), and Nivedita. In 1902, invited to Baroda by the Prince, Nivedita had met Sri Aurobindo and had told him that Bengal waited for him. Barin Ghose, Aurobindo's brother and collaborator, joined Banerjee to consolidate his mission. As a tribute to the doctrine of self-perfection (*anushilan*) chalked out by Bankim, a central revolutionary Party was constituted in Calcutta under the name of Anushilan, with secret units functioning all over the country. Other than intensive training in physical education, the militants attended classes in political, social and economic history, with discussions on the activist teaching of the *Gita*, around the central problem—the unconditional liberation of India. These classes were conducted by eminent specialists of respective domains—they anticipated the National Council of Education founded in 1906, with Sri Aurobindo as its principal, and Rabindranath Tagore, Sir Gurudas Banerjee, Rash Behari Ghose, Asutosh Chaudhuri, Surendranath Banerjee, Brajen Seal, A. Rasul, Satish Mukherjee, Taraknath Palit, Subodh Mallik, Brajendrakishore Raychaudhuri, among its professors and active members. It was the first organisation to welcome the Extremist revolutionary project conceived by Sri Aurobindo.

This extremist programme adopted notably by Tilak in Maharashtra, by Lajpat Rai in Punjab, and by Bipinchandra Pal in Bengal, had for goal: (1) Kindling the national spirit based on an unconditional independence of India (*swaraj*); (2) Launching a secret revolutionary action to prepare the youth, without losing sight of a possible phase of very

Lala Lajpat Rai, Lokmanya Tilak and Bipinchandra Pal (Lal-Bal-Pal)

controlled and temporary violence, to the extent of self-sacrifice in the name of the Motherland. A passive resistance would overtly accompany it and would drag the Indian mass progressively towards a collective involvement. The resistance would comprise:

(a) First, economic boycott of British products in order to encourage the industries and the national handicrafts (*svadeshi*), which were penalised by a policy of discrimination for the benefit of commodities imported from Great Britain: to assure a continuous adult education, open several technological schools in rural areas;

(b) Second, boycott of universities with English education,

in favour of instituting a parallel system of national education;

(c) Lastly, boycott the judiciary with the opening of national law courts.

Madness

In a letter to his wife, Mrinalini Devi, Sri Aurobindo clarified in 1905 his three "madnesses": (1) believe that all individual acquisitions only belong to God and must be necessarily at His service; (2) if God exists, there must be means to feel His Presence, to meet Him; however difficult be the path, he is determined to follow it; Hindu religion teaches that the path is to be discovered within: He is there inside the body, inside the mind; this religion gives us the necessary indications which he has begun to follow; after one month of practice, he has the experience that whatever Hindu religion teaches is not false: with the experience of given symptoms, he is busy passing through them; (3) the others know their Motherland as an inert matter, a cluster of fields, meadows, forests, mountains and rivers; he knows her as Mother, he worships her, he adores her; when an ogre sits on a mother's chest and is about to suck her blood, what does her son do? Does he sit down at the table and eat his lunch peacefully, pass his leisure with wife and children, or rush to rescue his mother? Sri Aurobindo knew that there is in him the necessary force to raise this fallen nation; it is not any physical force; he was not going to fight carrying a sword or a rifle; it is the force of Knowledge; the warrior's energy—*kshatra teja*—is not the only thing; there is also the sage's energy—*brahma teja*—that is seated on Knowledge; all this is not new to him; it is not the very day either that he felt it thus; it is with this faith that he was born and it is the marrow of his being; the Divine sent him in order to accomplish this great task; the seed had begun to germinate when he was fourteen years old, at eighteen years it had shot up firmly, ineradicably; he does not say that the mission was to be accomplished in his life-time, but it has to come true, he has the certitude about it.

Agitations in Bengal

The government's decision, in 1905, to divide Bengal into two States and to introduce a breach between the Hindus and the Muslims—having the immediate goal to frustrate the mass involvement—shook the whole of India with a spontaneous popular indignation. An indignation that brought all patriots (Moderates and Extremists) closer together. The Congress became the springboard, as it accelerated the programme of passive resistance under Tilak's leadership, supported by Aurobindo. Since 1906, as editor-in-chief of the *Bande Mataram*—English organ of the Extremists—Sri Aurobindo steeped his pen in vitriol, before attacking the abject politics of British in India. Reproduced simultaneously in the vernacular written press all over India, quoted in the British press (such as the *Times* of London), analysed before the Parliament, Aurobindo's articles became the manifesto of the militant nationalism of New India. A first trial against the *Bande Mataram* in August 1907 carried from country to country the name of this Prophet who preferred working from the backstage. Acquitted, he was welcomed by Tagore—in a public homage, his poem proclaimed Aurobindo as the Voice, incarnate and free, of the Motherland,

Lokmanya Tilak

> *The radiant Messenger who descended with God's lamp, what king can reach him, with what chain, what sceptre?*

H.W. Nevinson, an active member of the British political domain, was sent by the *Manchester Guardian* in December 1907, to interview Aurobindo. Acknowledging the Partition to be the greatest blessing for rousing India so suddenly from the age-old lethargy. By applying an over-all *swadeshi*—"not limited to goods but including every phase of life"—the Extremists were preparing the country for self-government, possibly like a State within the State. Having tasted a spiritual elevation in Aurobindo's presence, Nevinson remarked Aurobindo's religious tone, a spiritual elevation in his words, and held that nationalism for him was a duty superior to all political end. In the name of nationalism, a celestial ray gushed out of his look. "Grave with intensity, careless of fate or opinion, and one of the most silent of men I have known; he is of the stuff that dreamers are made of, but dreamers who act their dreams, indifferent to the means."[51] The British educator A.B. Clark of Baroda remembered this visionary colleague, "If Joan of Arc heard celestial voices, Aurobindo's eyes perceive divine visions."

Since Jatin Mukherjee met Sri Aurobindo, in 1903, two parallel tendencies appeared within the Extremist movement: (a) One, highly centralised under the authority of his own brother Barin Ghose—first of all, with Jatin's collaboration, Barin had started an experimental factory at Deoghar to manufacture rudimentary grenades by moulding shells; then, having for headquarters the garden house at Maniktola (Calcutta), in addition to the aforementioned activities, Barin had installed there a laboratory for more advanced explosives and, notably, of bombs; Hem Das, one of his associates, had just returned from Paris where he acquired some experience, in company of Safransky, chief of a Russian nihilist group. Barin's inclination for an untimely terrorism led this preparatory phase to a sudden end. (b) The other, decentralized and clandestine federation of a multitude of regional units that Jatin Mukherjee had founded, directly under Vivekananda's influence, shortly before 1900. Jatin encouraged free contacts between the leaders of these two currents: several of his close associates continued to execute Barin's orders.[52]

At the end of a terrorist manoeuvre, in April 1908, one of Barin's emissaries—Khudiram Bose—got arrested by the police, whereas his colleague Prafulla Chaki committed suicide. This event triggered a wave of massive incarcerations, including Tilak, Aurobindo and Barin (with residents of his headquarters at Maniktola). The government initiated the historic trial of the *Alipore Bomb* case, accompanied by more and more ferocious repressive measures, persuaded that the indictment of some revolutionaries would be sufficient to quench the rise of the militant nationalism. Imperturbable before this enormous grinding machine, between 1908 and 1910, Jatin Mukherjee set out reassembling the secret units and put a vast anti-repressive operation underway to prove before the country and before the authorities that the nationalists' resources remained intact—some spectacular hold-ups helped Jatin to finance the defence of the patriots under trial; the public murder of high grade police officers considerably foiled the colonial intentions. Again, Sri Aurobindo was discharged through lack of evidence in 1909, whereas, struck by a momentary defeatism, Barin and his followers admitted guilt and were sentenced to lifelong deportation to the Andamans.

The year spent in jail—in company of the Upanishads and the Gita, in practising intensive Hatha Yoga and meditation—opened before Sri Aurobindo perspectives beyond the immediate preoccupations of India's political liberation. A gamut of spiritual experiences guided him more and more to a universal consciousness. Persuaded that the movement of independence would henceforth follow its own course in the right direction, Sri Aurobindo proceeded to a new phase of his life. The achievement of his political objective indicated the beginning of man's spiritual liberation through the transformation of human nature. Having explained his new orientation during about eight months through two new magazines—the *Karmayogin* (in English) and *Dharma* (in Bengali)—Sri Aurobindo affirmed that he chose as a rule to follow the implicit direction within and to act only when the Divine made him act.

Reclusion in Pondicherry

Obeying instructions of an inner voice, in February 1910, Sri Aurobindo left Calcutta to arrive at Pondicherry on 4 April 1910, after having confided the editing of the *Karmayogin* to Nivedita. During the years that followed, till the last day of his life (5 December 1950), Sri Aurobindo would no more have any direct political activities, in spite of several invitations—even coming from Gandhi—to accept the Presidency of the National Congress. In spite of several repeated solicitations from the leaders representing the people's expectation, he remained firm in this decision. On 29 May 1928, after his meeting with Sri Aurobindo, Tagore wrote a long article from Pondicherry: "Finally I met Aurobindo Ghose again." On 15 August 1947, the day of his seventy-fifth birthday, Sri Aurobindo saw India celebrating her independence. On that day, in his message to the Nation broadcast by All India Radio, he spoke of five dreams of his life: (a) a revolutionary movement creating a free and united India; (b) the resurgence and liberation of the peoples of Asia; (c) a world union; (d) the spiritual gift of India to the world; (e) a step in evolution raising man to a higher and larger consciousness.

Poet, philosopher, spiritual master, much like a meteor, Sri Aurobindo passed through India's socio-political sky that, ever since, in spite of numerous influences, always cherishes the luminous imprint of an esoteric and spiritual nationalism that he bequeathed. Gandhi had but the choice of taking over from his precursors, among whom Sri Aurobindo represents the most important and most decisive personality.

The Last of the Prophets

Singling out in Sri Aurobindo "the noblest representative of the great neo-Vedantic spirit", Romain Rolland listened to his "voice, re-emerging out of Vivekananda's pyre. It is the same conception of a national ideal for India, identical to his spiritual mission. It is the same universal aspiration (...) The former political leader of revolted Bengal, who became the greatest thinker of today's India, accomplishes the most complete synthesis that has yet been attained between the genius of the West and the genius of the East(...) An Aurobindo Ghose blazing with a peerless faith in the unlimited powers of the soul and in human progress(...) thus becomes the perfect fusion of the most complete knowledge with the most intense action (...) and the last of her (India's) great Rishis holds in his hands the bow of the creative Impetus, ready to shoot in the air. It is an uninterrupted stream that flows from the farthest Yesterdays towards the farthest Tomorrows. The whole spiritual life of history is but one: *the One who advances...*"[53]

Rabindranath Tagore would write on Sri Aurobindo, after their last meeting, in Pondicherry, 29 May 1928: "At the very first sight I could realise that he had been seeking for the soul and had gained it, and through this long process of realisation had accumulated within him a silent power of inspiration. His face was radiant with an inner light... I felt that the utterance of the ancient Hindu Rishi spoke from him of that equanimity which gives the human soul its freedom of entrance into the All. I said to him: 'You have the Word and we are waiting to receive it from you. India will speak through your voice, *Hearken unto me*.'"[54]

A century before Sri Aurobindo, Rammohun Roy had founded a Unitarian Society composed of eminent Indian and European members, whose activities were followed with interest by Jeremy Bentham in England and Abbot Henri Gregoire in France. From his Persian treatise on the monists' quest, Rammohun had visualised, in 1828, the Brahma-Sabha, to welcome people eager to meet in an "orderly, sober, religious and devout manner" and in "the contemplation of the Author and Preserver of the Universe". Its object was "the promotion of charity, morality, piety, benevolence, virtue and the strengthening of the bonds of union between men of all religious pursuations and creeds."[55] In short, a forum of the cosmic Religion, promoter of a spiritual fraternity of mankind. By his own profession of faith—in the name of human unity—accomplished thanks to man's union with the Divine, Sri Aurobindo gave back to Rammohun's initial vision its title of glory and, while acting like a springboard, he invited men to attempt the somersault towards their Supramental future. It is probably an apotheosis of this vision that would appear in the dream of Auroville—its identity has to be first located in human psyche, before it can find a material existence. A place which no nation could claim as its own. A place where the needs of the mind and the aspirations of progress would excel beyond all personal passions and desires.

CHAPTER IV

BAGHA JATIN
(1879-1915)

CHAPTER IV

BAGHA JATIN (1879-1915)

Introduction

Devendranath Tagore owned the vast estate of Birhampore in the district of Nadia, with Shilaidaha as its headquarters. Ramsundar Chatterjee and Naimuddin Mian, respectively landlords of adjacent Koya and Kaloa, managed with much humanity the Hindu and the Muslim subjects of the Tagores. Ramsundar was most popular for his physical and moral courage, and esteemed for his skill and experience. At the age of seventy-five, in 1870, he gave his granddaughter Sharat Shashi (1858-1899) in marriage to Umesh Chandra Mukherjee (1850-1884), living in the village Sadhuhati Rishkhali, in Jhenaidah, the neighbouring subdivision belonging to Jessore. Umesh owned some lands and spent his time studying the scriptures and looking after his horses. When on horse-back he visited the country-side; even the arrogant indigo-planters hailed him courteously. Umesh regularly received books and periodicals from Calcutta. His wife was fond of their library where elegantly bound copies of *Banga-darshan* edited by Bankim Chandra, *Arya-darshan* by Yogendra Vidyabhushan and *Bharati* by the Tagores found their place by the side of essays, novels and poems by contemporary Bengali authors. Vinodebala, the first child of this happy couple, was born in 1974, with the publication of the *Arya-darshan*; two years earlier, the issuing of the *Banga-darshan* had seemed to be as important in the people's life as that of the *Encyclopedia* preceding the revolution in France.[56] The year 1879—when Jatindranath Mukherjee ("Bagha Jatin") was born, a century after the French Revolution—roused a new enthusiasm with the coming out of the collected essays of Bankim Chandra. A few months later, advised by Surendranath Banerjee, Yogendra took to inspiring readers with his bestseller biographies of Mazzini, Garibaldi and other revolutionaries to incite the people to sacrifice themselves for the Motherland. He said, "I shall be fulfilled if even a single reader takes the decision of sacrificing his own interest in the interest of the Nation."[57]

A Mother's Ambition

Daughter of Nadia—a district hallowed with the cult of Love taught by Shri Chaitanya—Sharat Shashi acquired an inner plenitude in her life in Jessore, particularly known for its heroic tradition. A born poet, spirited, generous, skilful in her household chores and artistic activities, she conducted workshops with ladies of the vicinity and was awarded distinctions by cultural associations for her social initiatives. As soon as she heard of anyone suffering in the neighbourhood, she rushed to nurse the sick. When Jatindra was hardly five, he lost his father. Invited by her grandfather and her elder brothers, Sharat Shashi returned to her parents' home in Koya, with Vinodebala, Jatindra and his little brother Surendra. This child was named after Surendra Tagore, nephew of the poet Rabindranath and a close friend of the family. Following Surendra's sudden death, Vinodebala became widow and returned to Koya, too. Drawing an incandescent inspiration from all this tragedy, Sharat Shashi was determined to bring up her children to conform to her deceased husband's god-loving ideals. An all-rounder in studies, in sports and in innocent pranks, Jatindra excelled also in playing roles of Hanuman, King Harish Chandra, Dhruva, Prahlad, Pratapaditya in dramatic performances. Jatindra's passion for the urban stage and the village operas was to help him choose them as adequate means for patriotic propaganda. Like a dexterous stage-manager, between 1908-1910 and, again, in 1915, he was to enact a dazzling pageant of fireworks all over the country, in form of an armed riposte to the colonial repressive measures. He, with a group of friends, founded a club where, in addition to theatre and football—Jatindra's second passion—, they sat discussing patriotic literature and the *Gita*; very soon Uncle Basanta Kumar, a pleader, and Surendra Tagore conducted classes for them on several subjects. In 1893, as a student of the famous A.V. School at Krishnagar, Jatindra saved the life of a boy by snatching him away from the trajectory of a mad horse and, tamed the animal by riding it.

On contracting the contagion while looking after a cholera patient, Sharat Shashi was to die at the age of forty-one.[58] That was to be the crowning lesson of devoted service she taught, instilling in her children the love for their society, their country, and their Creator.

Bagha Jatin

Calcutta Central College

After passing the Entrance in 1895, Jatindra joined the Calcutta College for his higher studies; it was situated midway between Swami Vivekananda's house, on one side, and that of Yogendra Vidyabhushan on the other—two of his mentors, two makers of the new generation. Welcomed by

Vivekananda, young Jatindra learnt that it is possible to lead a saintly life even for a family man dedicated to the service of the Motherland. Vivekananda advised him to concentrate on self-improvement (*anushilan*, as preconised by Bankim Chandra) and sent him to the gymnasium of Ambu Guha where the Swami himself practised the traditional Indian wrestling. At this gymnasium—a cross-road of great minds—Jatindra came across people like Shashibhushan Raychaudhuri (the educationist popularly known as "Shashi-da") and Sachin Banerjee, son of Yogendra who at once singled out Jatindra as a significant guest. On a wall inside his drawing room, Yogendra showed Vivekananda's inscription that India was to win her freedom in 1925![59] In 1903, when Sri Aurobindo went to stay with Yogendra, the latter introduced him to Jatindra who was to be recognized by Sri Aurobindo as his "right-hand man". Nivedita is said to have been happy with this meeting.

Shortly before the final examination at the Calcutta Central College, fed up with the system of education of an imperialist State, Jatindra had given up his studies. The Dawn Society under Satish Mukherjee was created in 1905 as a nursery of patriotism to provide a training ground for youths. It had become one of the most active centres for the propagation of boycott-*Swadeshi* ideologies. In tune with the programme of a new pedagogy introduced by Sri Aurobindo, the Society's object was to awaken students to the needs of the country, to love Mother India, to cultivate their moral character, to think for themselves. It had a weekly session for "general training course". In addition to Satish's ardent message of philanthropy rousing the youth to dedicated service, they would also follow Pandit Nilakantha Goswami's talks on the *Gita*, impressing on the listeners' mind the futility of life and death; teaching them that the only thing that counted was duty and right action. Celebrities like Sister Nivedita, Jatin Mukherjee (Bagha Jatin), Dr. Rajendra Prasad, Radhakumud Mukherjee, Benoykumar Sarkar attended classes at the "Dawn".[60]

Lessons from the Swami

First and foremost, Vivekananda had taught Jatindra the secret of containing and controlling the seminal energy (*brahmacharya*), leading to a purity and an altitude in action and thought, source of an immense physical and mental strength—a married man can also attain this state by remaining steadfast to his wife, procreate without lust, and desire no other women. Jatindra's exemplary integrity drew even the admiration of observers like the English Superintendent of Police, J.E. Armstrong who wrote in his report that Jatindra "owed his prominent position in revolutionary circles, not only to his quality of leadership, but in great measure to his reputation of being a *Brahmachari* with no thought beyond the revolutionary cause."[61] On the foil of reports concerning various deviations from other leaders, this was a timely tribute. His followers saw in him almost a perfect man, having forged his innate qualities according to the stern principles of self-making (*anushilan*): "His very life was in tune with the *Gita*. Happiness and suffering, living and dying, gain and loss, censure and praise were all equal for him.[62] Others have identified in him the unconditional surrender—as described by Vivekananda and Sri Aurobindo—, compatible only with a mighty personality of Jatindra's stature; he was looked up on as the divinised pioneer of the integral yoga.[63]

Brought up by a mother particularly dedicated to social service, Jatindra had more than a predisposition for charitable gestures. Step by step the Swami revealed to him the utility of serving the suffering fellow creatures, before undertaking an armed insurrection for the political freedom (*mukti*) of India. For both these missions, he was to *make men* who, instead of yearning for personal release and deliverance (*moksha*) would be prepared for the cause of the Motherland. Vivekananda's "Die in the name of an ideal" assumed in Jatindra's motto: "We shall die to arouse the Nation."

The Swami was to advocate a heroic attitude in front of the enemy. In the *Bharati*, in 1880, Rabindranath had recognised that since our childhood the cult of fear has impressed on our mind fear as our lord, fear as our ruler; we fail to obey anything other than fear: "Is this the method of acquiring independence?"[64] In the course of this article, he had suggested without hesitation:

> "Many think that there is no better remedy to tyranny than the clenched fist; indeed those who, having diagnosed the state of the sick, pretend nevertheless, to behave as civilized Christians, while worshipping brutal power; those who do not shrink from blandly applying physical force against the helpless and do not count it as an act of cowardice; playfully, those who can kill the coloured people; will they accept any other antidote than the vigorous clenched fist?...We must assist the natives as best as possible in quenching the English tyranny. We must veritably learn to sacrifice our selfish ends for the good of our compatriots, instead of merely wagging our tongues. We must realise that the danger which threatens our compatriots under foreign hands is for us a humiliation."[65]

Four years later, he had raised the question, after having analyzed the rulers' mentality: "Do they recognize any other lesson than that of the clenched fist ?" In reply to Bipinchandra's article[66] in 1903 discussing the problem of the English tyranny in India, Rabindranath asked in his article, "Boxing Bout" (*ghushoghushi*), whether it was indispensable for innocent Indians—victims of the conceited Englishmen's behaviour—to return tit for tat. Absolutely sanguine about the utility of a well served slap in return for a blow with the fist, he did not fail to warn that in case an individual Englishman is personally thrashed by a native citizen, the entire English community flares up as a collective insult and turns it into a matter of sedition. Henceforth, to fight against them, Indians require a collective preparation. This reminds us that since meeting Sri Aurobindo in 1903, Jatindra had set to transform his gymnastic clubs into secret branches of the revolutionary Anushilan in various districts.

The secret preparations had also an overt counterpart. Already well-known for distributing adequate lessons to arrogant English army officers, Jatindra was informed about the plans of the government to invite the Prince of Wales to an Indian tour with a view to appease the agitations against the Partition of Bengal in 1905. Jatindra decided to enact before the future Emperor a first-hand show of the way the HM's officers humiliated the natives. With the procession approaching, Jatindra singled out a cabriolet on a side-lane, very near the Royal coach—a batch of English military men seated on its roof, had been dangling their booted legs against the windows where there were some Bengali ladies, their faces livid. Requesting the fellows to leave the ladies alone, in reply to their vulgar provocation, Jatindra rushed up to the roof and felled the officers with pure Bengali slaps till they dropped off on the ground. The Prince, on his return from the Indian tour, had several discussions with Morley about "the ungracious bearing of Europeans to Indians."[67]

Certainly on gathering from Vivekananda the anecdote about the handloom, while looking after the Poragacha unit (Nadia), in 1905 Jatindra inspired his friend Amarendra Chatterjee (1880-1957) to take it up as an immediate preoccupation. Sponsored by Raja Pyarimohan Mukherjee, Amarendra bought six handlooms and set to hawking homespun textile. He, Jatindra and other associates got the *Chhatra Bhandar* ("Students' Emporium") registered during the anti-Partition agitations. It was going to be a prosperous enterprise leading to the creation of Amarendra's *Shramajivi Samavaya* ("Working Men's Cooperative"). Behind the apparent commercial activities, these stores served as meeting places of the leaders and shelters for militants coming from the districts. In 1908-09, when the colonial repressive measures tried to throttle increasingly all seditious activities, following the example of Jyotirindra Tagore, Jatindra got registered the Bengal Young Men's Cooperative Credit and Zamindari Society with the help of Surendra Tagore and others, leased from Sir Daniel Hamilton a few acres of land at Gosaba. In addition to boarding and lodging militants who had escaped the police persecution, he helped them to open night classes for adults and polytechnic schools as experimented by Shashida thanks to a direct guidance from Vivekananda, set up Ayurvedic and homoeopathic dispensaries and small-scale cottage industries, clubs for physical training. By picking up competent associates, he taught them shooting in the marshes. Together with Amarendra, Jatindra was seen organising volunteers with a military discipline during large religious congregations. In his confidential Report 1907-1917, James Campbell Ker (Indian Civil Service)—retracing the evolution of Extremism—admitted that in 1907 the militants of Bengal, in addition to setting fire to foreign goods and attending political gatherings, went to the great fairs and the religious communities to facilitate the life of the participants and pilgrims. "It is interesting to note that on several occasions their interventions were very useful, notably—as the Bengali press goes on hammering—at the time of the Ardhodaya Yoga in Calcutta in February 1908. It was a religious festival that attracted thousands of pilgrims from all corners of Bengal and about one thousand simple volunteers and two hundred doctors were on the spot. Since the organisers had for goal to prove that that the militants were not only innocuous but, moreover, useful—they and their exemplary behaviour have been congratulated even by the Commissioner of Police. Their presence in these places served three purposes: to offer to the youth a training in organisation; to revive the popular militant movement; to insinuate before the public that the performance of the militants was superior to that of the Police. This English administrator cites an excerpt of the *Bande Mataram* of 7 March 1908, concerning a pilgrimage in Chittagong: "The organisation was a perfect success, and for some days it was as if the government of the Sitakunda had come into the hands of the Volunteers, composed of pleaders, doctors and traders (...) Pilgrims were heard saying that when *Bande Mataram* has come there is no fear (...) The Police acted in cooperation, and helped the work of the Volunteers."[68]

During Sri Aurobindo's trial in the *Alipore Bomb* case, in 1909, having met at New York Bhupendranath Datta (Swamiji's brother), Nivedita had commented: "Even though the capital punishments dogs Aurobindo, he cares a twopence for it." Returning from her Western tour to India in July 1909, "Nivedita was delighted that Sri Aurobindo was free again and she promptly organised celebrations in her school. And she wondered at the marvellous change—the transformation—that had come over Sri Aurobindo. His face seemed to be all eyes and little else, eyes burning with the intensity and power that had become his during his *sadhana* in prison."[69] Later Sri Aurobindo confessed that while in prison, he plunged in Nirvana—"with that peace one does not ask for anything"—it was the spirit of Vivekananda that first gave him "a clue in the direction of the Supermind".[70] When Sri Aurobindo was again to be prosecuted, Nivedita mentioned: "The leader at a distance can work as much as at home."[71] Before leaving for Pondicherry via Chandernagore, in 1910, regretting that Jatindra was still in prison, Sri Aurobindo left his instruction: "Follow Jatin."[72] In a conversation, Gourkishore Ghose informed the present writer that, temporarily upset by Sri Aurobindo's withdrawal from politics, in 1910, Nivedita had told Saralabala Sarkar that Jatindra Mukherjee was indeed the most trustworthy and consistent among the active revolutionary leaders.

Atul Krishna Ghose

In July 1913, Jatin with his old friend Amarendra and two associates (Atul Krishna Ghose and Karunamoy Sarkar)—all very close to the Sri Ramakrishna Mission—left for organising relief for the victims of the Damodar flooding the districts of Burdwan, Hughli and Midnapore. W. Sealy did not fail to detect that "cloaked under the guise of philanthropy, these bands of young men were as a matter of fact sent with the main objective of spreading discontent, embarrassing government officials by minimising their work and poisoning the minds of the peasantry by spreading known of the malicious stories as to the real cause of the floods."[73] Other revolutionary leaders such as Satish Basu and Kiran Mukherjee of the Calcutta Anushilan, Makhanlal Sen of the Dhaka Anushilan, Ramchandra Majumdar, Jnanendra Banerjee, Rasiklal Datta, Sushil Mitra came to join them very soon. According to the Nixon Report, impressed by the sincerity of these first-aid workers, Motilal Ray, coming to observe on the spot, in September, proposed to send some emissaries to Professor Charu Chandra Ray in Chandernagore to collect funds.

In another confidential note (dated 22 April 1914) on Sri Ramakrishna Mission, having described the Extremist leaders' care to shelter this organisation from political controversy, Charles Tegart provided the list of revolutionaries of a dangerous character who frequented Belur, near Calcutta, or its different branches all over India: right from Sri Aurobindo, Jatin Mukherjee, Amarendra Chatterji, Makhan Sen, Upendra Banerjee, Rishikesh Kanjilal, Kunjalal Saha, Bhababhushan Mitra, Debabrata Basu, Sachin Sen, and so many others were blacklisted here. Amarendra and Makhan seemed to found branches of this establishment wherever the police saw them busy with their nationalist activity. Saradananda, the Mission's Secretary, recognised having advanced important subsidies to Amarendra for the Damodar relief fund. To celebrate Sri Ramakrishna's birthday at Belur, on 1 March (1914), in presence of a very big assembly, in addition to Amarendra and Makhan (already mentioned), Jatindranath Mukherjee and other eminent members of the revolutionary party, were seen serving food to the poor and helping the monastery authorities by taking care of the guests. Amarendra had come with a great number of volunteers on this occasion. While underlining that the brother of Sarat Chandra Chakravarti (1865-1927) alias Swami Saradananda was an active and dangerous revolutionary, Tegart affirmed how easy it was to demonstrate that many passages of Swami Vivekananda's writings are pregnant with insurrection, that their potentialities of damages had reached their climax, the revolutionary party making full use of it.[74]

The thirst with which young Jatindra had approached Vivekananda for guidance in life was as eager as the impatience for realizing God which led Narendra Datta to Sri Ramakrishna. Neither in his service for relieving the miserable fellow creatures, nor in his hectic engagement to prepare the compatriots for a decisive struggle to free India did Jatindra forget the spiritual mission he had received from Vivekananda. Questioned by a disciple whether liberation (*mukti*) of the Motherland was compatible with ultimate Deliverance (*moksha*), Vivekananda had assured that *mukti* was the immediate and only path leading to *moksha*. For the time being, forgetting about all other divinities, Jatindra instructed his followers to worship only Mother India, as advised by Vivekananda. Approached by young Chittapriya Raychaudhuri whether revolutionary activities were truly compatible with spiritual quest, Jatindra was to reply that he at least would not have been there, had it not been so.

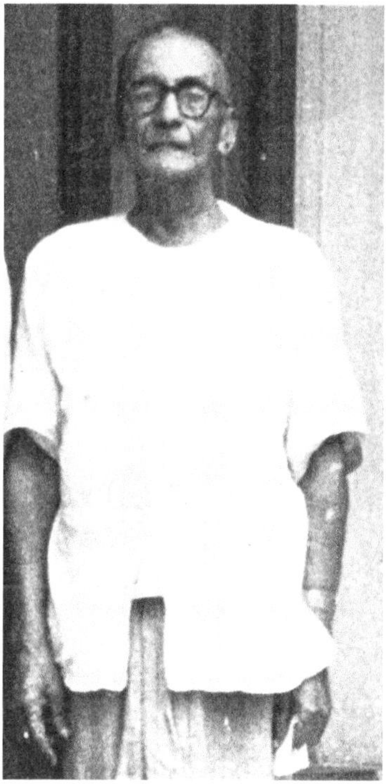

Nalinikanta Kar

According to Nalinikanta Kar during the months preceding his self-sacrifice, in his hide-out in the forest of Kaptipoda, every day before the sunset, a handful of revolutionary followers surrounding their Dada, Jatindra held a class on the *Gita*: "The Gita was the ideal of his life... When Dada recited the Gita with his sonorous voice, his trance-lost face beamed with a rare glow. We felt ecstatic by contemplating that face. We felt as if Gautam Muni in person was chanting Vedic hymns. A peaceful meditation seemed to engulf the tranquil forest resort. Even though we did not fully understand the message of the *Gita*, we would get lost, however, in an ineffable joy at the sight of that serene silhouette. Tears pervaded our eyes."[75]

Another eye witness, Manindra Chakravarti, was sitting near him at sunset. Manindra kept quiet when suddenly Jatindra became silent. On watching Jatindra's contemplative face and mysterious look, Manindra found him wrapped in ecstasy... His gaze was fixed on the top of a tall *sal* tree. An immobility of a statue. All of a sudden, catching hold of Manindra's hand, Jatindra exlaimed: "Look there, look at my Krishna!" Unable to perceive anything, Manindra felt an electrifying current of joy transmitted all over his body by that very touch. "Blessed you are, Jatin, blessed your life," were the final words jotted down by Manindra.[76]

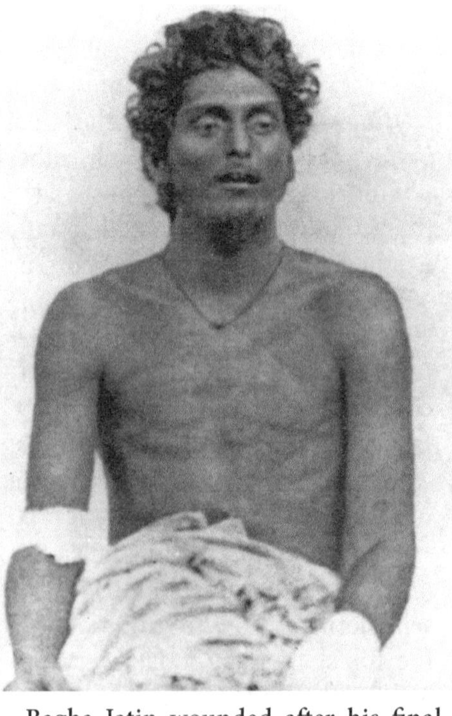

Bagha Jatin wounded after his final battle at the banks of Burha Balang, off Balasore.

"Die for an ideal, since die we must," was Vivekananda's advice to Jatindra. Most probably Vivekananda himself had never imagined the glorious death Jatindra was to choose on 9 September 1915, with four brave young followers—Chittapriya, Niren Dasgupta, Manoranjan Sengupta and Jyotish Pal—in a pitched battle against an armed detachment. Even observers on the imperial side admired the blazing picture of this first guerilla war fought in modern times, on the very soil of India. The Phoenix of revolution emerged out of that pyre to lead a generation of desperate volunteers for freeing the Motherland to its cherished phase of the mass movement.

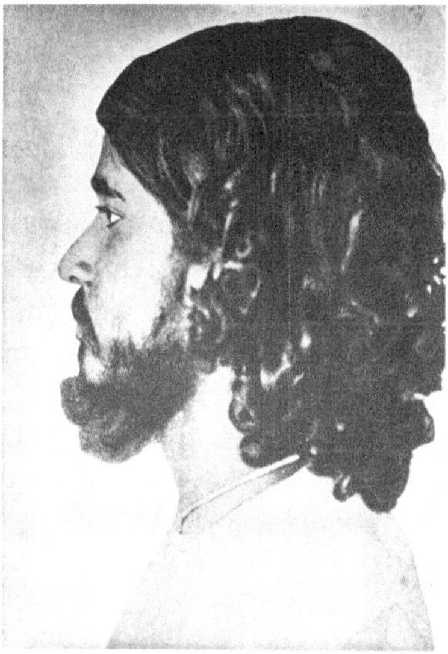
Naren Bhattacharya (M.N. Roy)

A Reason-proof God

Two of Jatindra's followers—Harikumar Chakravarti and Naren Bhattacharya (future M.N. Roy)—had grasped, thanks to Jatindra, how profound was Vivekananda's conviction that it was possible to lead a saintly life without donning necessarily the garb of a monk; it was a heroic challenge, indeed. Accepting the Swami's Advaita Vedanta teaching, Harikumar stopped worshipping images and believing in God, whereas Naren stuck to both. According to Harikumar, the Swami held that there was no God; Naren was sanguine that the Swami believed in God's existence. Requested to settle this theological dilemma, Jatindra preferred taking them to his Guru, Bholanand Giri of Haridwar, who was on a visit to Calcutta. After listening to the object of their debate, Giriji told Harikumar: "You are right, my Son. There is no God." Then, turning to Naren he assured: "God does exist." Then he added: "Let everybody live according to his own opinion." Later, dissatisfied with this enigmatic reply, the two opponents turned to Jatindra, seeking a solution. Jatindra consoled them by telling them how great Vivekananda's thoughts were and how futile it was to dispute

Har Dayal

his words: "If India chose to listen to Vivekananda, there will be no end to her glory."[77]

Like Taraknath Das, Adhar Laskar, Satyen Sen, Guran Ditt Kumar, Darisi Chenchiah and a few others, Jiten Lahiri—one of *Jugantar* emissaries—was enrolled at Berkeley, studying Organic Chemistry and making explosives; all of them were eager to get military training, as wished by Jatindra. In January 1913, while attending with Chenchia one of Har Dayal's lectures on Indian philosophy, he was startled by the lecturer's sudden vehemence in treating Vivekananda as an escapist. Lahiri taxed Dayal mercilessly with sheer escapism, turning his back, unawares, to the determination of millions of Indian emigrants in the USA who had been waiting for a proper leadership to fight for India's freedom. Taken aback, Dayal resigned from his post at the University, discovered the formidable Federation of Patriots, with branches active all over North America and Canada: the prototype of the future Gadhar movement. He sent a telegram to his mentor Taraknath Das to come over from New York.[78]

Taraknath Das

Conclusion

Having met men who mattered in the twentieth century—

men like Lenin, Stalin, Ho Chi Minh—M.N. Roy described them as *great men* and Jatindra to be a *good man*; Roy further specified: "Good men are seldom given a place in the galaxy of the great. It will continue to be so until goodness is recognised as the measure of genuine greatness. Jatin-da was not the embodiment of the medieval values of war-likeness and heroism. He did not belong to any age; his values were human and as such transcended space and time, He was kind and truthful as well as bold and uncompromising. His boldness stopped short of cruelty, and his uncompromisingness did not preclude toleration. Like all modern educated young men of his time, he tended to accept the reformed religion preached by Swami Vivekananda—a God who would stand the test of reason, and a religion which served progressive social and human purpose. He believed himself to be a *Karmayogi*, trying to be at any rate, and recommended the ideal to all of us. Detached from the unnecessary mystic preoccupation, *Karmayogi* means a humanist. He who believes that self-realisation can be attained through human action, must logically also believe in man's creativeness—that man is the maker of his destiny. That is also the essence of Humanism. Jatin-da was a Humanist—perhaps the first in modern India. To recognise him as such will be the most befitting homage to his memory."[79]

Struck by the degree of Jatindra's assimilation of Vivekananda's teachings, some historians have observed a strange resemblance—as much physical as psychical—between them; both appeared to have been moulded by the same divine artisan: "If Vivekananda chose to be Jatindra, he could as well do it, and the reverse".[80]

CHAPTER V

Had Bagha Jatin Succeeded: A Nationalist Revolt in Colonial India During World War I

CHAPTER V

Had Bagha Jatin Succeeded: A Nationalist Revolt in Colonial India During World War I [81]

While in Europe begins the commemoration of the First World War, in India we are approaching the centenary of the heroic self-giving of Jatindranath Mukherjee, popularly known as Bagha Jatin ("Valorous like a Tiger")—at the age of thirty-five. On 9 September 1915 he with four brave comrades fought up to their last bullet, against a detachment of armed police, before succumbing. Their short life and their glorious death thus preceded and prepared the movement of the mass that Gandhi was predestined to lead.

In the foreword of a Bengali biography of Bagha Jatin, Dr. Syamaprasad Mookerjee had penned in 1947: "The young Bengali revolutionaries had written a blood-red chapter of their country's fight for freedom. Sacrificing all they had, once upon a time they had rushed to the ritual call of death and, inch by inch, by shedding their lives, they had left for us the relish of a greater life. Unfortunately, today we have forgotten most of them; even their names have been almost obliterated from the memory of the present generations. In the pages of history, neither at home nor abroad has this story been properly presented; the historians' pen has till now been terrorised by fear of the rulers, fear of the society, and scruple for superstition.

Most of those who were pioneers in that revolutionary movement are no more. In silence and without anyone's knowledge, those who had pledged their quest of freedom had never wished to drag their glorious deeds out of the caverns of secrecy for informing everybody in the broad daylight. Once the element of their quest turned important for history, a few of them, surviving, have tried to preserve those elements in form of stray and corrupt memoirs. That memorable yet very little-known history of the epoch in question remains hidden in proceedings of various trials for political conspiracies, most of them in form of Secret Papers of the then government. Probably for some more years those documents will not be available for historical research. Although in the form of books and essays, in the form of certain short stories and novels there have been attempts made to expose to Bengali readers the history of the revolutionary doctrine of Bengal but, from the point of view of facts, it remains—in most of the cases—mere fragments, incomplete; moreover half-diluted in fiction, a certain romantic imagination has been the outgrowth around this movement. It is now time to collect earnestly whatever material we can concerning the utmost available biography of the leading revolutionary figures, their activities, their principles, their revolutionary methods, their vision of life and the ideology they put to practice in life.

"...Jatindranath" wrote Dr. Mookerjee, "was the well-known and principal leader of the second episode in the history of revolutionary movement. This little book represents an abridged yet exactly described story of his life and his action; a precious material for history. It will only be possible to write a global history of the revolutionary movement by collecting thus, bit by bit, all available material; and if such an endeavour is not undertaken immediately, much material will sink into the depths of oblivion."

It is time that we examine a few details about Bagha Jatin's policy and the role he was to play in history. During half a century since 1955, devoted to research on the life and the times of this legendary hero, the author had kept in mind as one of the guiding lines the above foreword by Dr. Mookerjee. After a long correspondence with and interviewing people who had known Bagha Jatin, thanks to Bhupendrakumar Datta, he explored the State and National Archives under a privileged condition, before consulting files in European and American archives. He has, by now, published a good number of books; two in Bengali: (a) *Sadhak biplabi Jatindranath*, West Bengal State Book Board, Calcutta (1991, reprinted 2013); (b) *Bagha Jatin*, Dey's Publishers from Calcutta (running several editions since 1991); two books in English : (a) *Undying Courage*, Academic Publishers from Calcutta (1985); (b) *Bagha Jatin*, National Book Trust, New Delhi (2010, reprinted 2013); in French the lengthy chapter "The Thinker in Action" (pp.109-172) in his thesis, *Intellectual Roots of Freedom Movement in India* (1893-1918), Codex Publications, 2010, foreword by Jacques Attali. Side by side, he published several articles and papers such as: (a) Proceedings of Indian History Records Commission, Mysore, February 1977; (b) Proceedings of Indian History Congress, Bhubaneswar, December, 1977; (c) Wikipedia (English and French editions) under the pen name Bob Clive.

Truly speaking, as mentioned by Jacques Attali, the non-violent movement for India's freedom launched by Gandhi between the two wars and after the Second World War had its roots in the actions—often radical—of his predecessors. During the First World War, Indian nationalists received indeed the support of German empire in form of arms and ammunitions sent to India from the Californian coast. Our research intends to explore the highlights of this project and pin-point the decisive role played by Bagha Jatin in this context. Fond of action in silence, he has been compared to those "whales that indwell the depths of the ocean, stirring the innermost core of society".[82] M.N. Roy wrote: "He must be appreciated as the archetypal man the like of whom, though not many, live and die apparently without leaving any foot-prints on the sands of time. But in reality, they embody rays of hope, breaking through the darkness of the mass of mediocrity, aggravated from time to time by the blinding flashes of the greatness of built-up personalities."[83]

Plan for an Insurrection

The first question that arises is: Bagha Jatin's plot, known to historians as the Indo-German Conspiracy (or the Zimmerman Plan) to import arms and ammunition from Germany via California, during World War I leaked out mostly from several fronts. Which were they?

Perfectly lucid about the immense degree of ambition he had injected into this plan which he knew, however, was likely to fail in the context of a country so long under bondage, Bagha Jatin was convinced that *thelay thelay jat jagbe*—only blow after blow, in succeeding phases, could help waking up the Nation in the long run. Simultaneously, he had been sending emissaries abroad to convince people of the world how urgent was India's will to win her independence from the colonial exploitation. Having conversed by correspondence and met most surviving colleagues of Bagha Jatin since 1955, I could summarise into three stages the revolution as he had conceived it:

(a) Individual martyrdom of an elite, to begin with.
(b) Then, skirmish and guerilla warfare.
(c) Finally, freed psychologically from the clutch of multiple hesitations and fears, prepared at last to sacrifice themselves in the name of the Motherland, the mass would know how to swell the ranks of a movement of the people for an insurrection.

Having perfectly sensed the multiple play of diffidence and duplicity inside the country and abroad, when Bagha Jatin came to know about the failure of the arms expedition, instead of lamenting over the shattering of so many years of painstaking labour, he is reported to have stated in a calm voice: "God has rectified our decision. We had wished to free India with another foreign power. But India has to rise with her own strength." When as a consolation, some daredevil associates proposed to carry on other attempts to import arms by land, Bagha Jatin—while going through the ominous newspaper cutting received from Penang—chuckled and said: "Country's salvation from within!"[84] This reminded everybody about his intimate wish: *amra morbo, jat jagbe*! ("We shall die [so that] the Nation wakes up").

We have to keep in view that since January 1910, for thirteen months Bagha Jatin had been an under-trial prisoner waiting for the verdict of the *Howrah Conspiracy* case which was launched to prove his role as the principal instigator of a revolution against the British Crown, with the participation of students, workers and, above all, native soldiers from various regiments of the Royal army. The two officers of the 10th Jats, Surjan Singh and Ramgopal—in charge of the Fort William of Calcutta, the vital centre of the security of the Empire—had been members of the secret society led by Bagha Jatin: his associates accompanied them to numerous barracks in Upper India. Extremist factions of the Arya Samaj, disciples of Swami Dayananda (1824-83) based at Benares, Nainital, Lahore, Peshawar, had already responded warmly to the revolutionary call of Jatin Banerjee (Swami Niralamba), friend of Bagha Jatin.

Even before his release, Bagha Jatin was informed by his emissaries abroad about the famous expectation of Friedrich von Bernhardi (1849-1930)—this German general, an eminent author, had been the Director of the history of war of the General Staff; promoted Commandant General of the 7th Division in

1909, he was disliked by Wilhelm II and other authorities for his book *Germany and the Next War* in which he predicted a war between Germany and Great Britain—he foresaw therein the great danger for England in its colonial interests owing to a possible fusion between Indian and Egyptian nationalists along with Pan-Islamism. J.C. Nixon, ICS, recognised how Bagha Jatin was quick in holding the oncoming war to be a splendid opportunity for his insurrection; hence for the year to come, he put a dramatical end to all violent riposte to government acts of repression.[85]

Home interned, Bagha Jatin managed to meet the German Crown Prince on visit to Calcutta and received from him the promise of arms delivery, in case of an uprising. In 1913, busy bringing relief to the flood-stricken areas on the Damodar river, Bagha Jatin organised secret meetings with his associates for a big action in the near future. At this juncture, he received also Rash Behari Bose (1886-1945)—absconding since his almost successful attempt to murder the Viceroy Hardinge at New Delhi. Bose received from Bagha Jatin the clear project of an insurrection of the 1857-style revolt of the sepoys. Having met in Jatin the "ideal leader of men", Bose consulted Sri Aurobindo and received his full consent in favour of his joining the plan that Bagha Jatin undertook.

Rash Behari Bose

Indian revolutionaries in Europe: the Zimmermann Plan

Shyamaji Krishnavarma

Welcomed by socialist friends like Henry Mayers Hyndman (1842-1921), founder of the Social Democratic Federation, in 1905, Shyamaji Krishnavarma (1857-1930), Indian patriot and disciple of Herbert Spencer, published from London the *Indian Sociologist* while he inaugurated India House to accommodate Indian students in a revolutionary climate. Shyamaji was assisted by young militants like V.V.S. Aiyar (1875-1925), V.D. Savarkar (1883-

Le Jugement de l'Affaire Savarkar

Dans son arrêt la Cour d'Arbitrage décide que Savarkar ne sera pas rendu. — La grâce se produira-t-elle ?

DAMODAR VINAYAK SAVARKAR

C'est avec un douloureux étonnement que nous avons appris, hier soir, la sentence rendue par la Cour d'Arbitrage dans l'affaire Savarkar.

Voici en quels termes, de La Haye, on nous fait connaître le regrettable arrêt :

« *Humanité* ». — *Paris*

La Haye, 24 *février*. — (Par dépêche de notre correspondant.) — *La Cour d'Arbitrage déclare que la Grande-Bretagne n'ayant pas eu recours à des manœuvres frauduleuses ou à des actes de violence pour rentrer en possession de Savarkar, son arrestation n'a pas porté atteinte à la souveraineté de la France.*

Elle ajoute « qu'en admettant qu'il y ait eu irrégularité, il n'existe pas de règle de droit international, en vertu de laquelle une puissance devrait rendre un prisonnier à raison d'une faute commise par l'agent étranger qui le lui a livré ».

Par conséquent, Savarkar ne doit pas être rendu à la France.

D'autre part, d'après la dépêche Havas l'arrêt déclarerait « qu'en admettant qu'une illégalité ait été commise, elle l'a été de bonne foi ».

Il est impossible de réunir dans une décision de justice autant d'affirmations inexactes et controuvées.

Dire qu'il n'y a pas eu « manœuvre frauduleuse » de la part des agents anglais, pour obtenir la remise de Savarkar, ajouter qu'elle a été opérée « de bonne foi », c'est simplement nier ou ignorer les circonstances de fait les moins contestables, les mieux établies.

Le gendarme Pesquié, il l'a dit et répété — et *personne ne l'a nié* — n'a remis Savarkar entre les mains des policiers hindous que parce que ceux-ci, suivant l'expression de la revue anglaise *Nation*, l'avaient TROMPE sur la véritable qualité du fugitif.

Les cris : « Au voleur ! » qui s'élevaient de la passerelle même du bateau anglais constituent la manœuvre frauduleuse la plus caractérisée. L'invitation du consul d'Angleterre priant Pesquié « d'empêcher la fuite des déserteurs maritimes » est une autre preuve de la mauvaise foi des fonctionnaires anglais dans toute cette affaire et des conditions frauduleuses dans lesquelles s'est opérée l'arrestation.

Nous reviendrons demain sur cet arrêt et nous ferons les réflexions qu'il peut inspirer.

Quoi qu'il en soit, il faut espérer que le gouvernement britannique ayant obtenu satisfaction pour son amour-propre et son orgueil « impérial », comprendra la nécessité d'une mesure gracieuse à l'égard de l'héroïque jeune révolutionnaire hindou — voué autrement à la « guillotine sèche » de cette Sibérie hindoue que sont les îles Andjuman. Le ministère libéral de M. Asquith s'honorerait hautement aux yeux de l'opinion universelle en prenant une semblable mesure à l'égard de Damodar Vinayak Savarkar.

Jean LONGUET.

Report on the Case at the Permanent Court, Hague, published in the French daily *L'Humanite* on 24 February 1911, signed by Jean Longuet, son-in-law of Karl Marx.

1966), Har Dayal (1884-1939), Tirumal Achari (1887-1951), Virendranath Chattopadhyay or "Chatto" (1880-1937*). Carrying the flame of Shyamaji to Paris, Madam Bhikhaji Cama (1861-1936) and Raoji Rana (1870-?**) created in Paris a similar home. As soon as the *Bande Mataram* edited by Sri Aurobindo from Calcutta ceased to appear, in 1908 Madam Cama launched a new journal, *Homonymous*, printed from Geneva, singing praise of Bengali martyrs like Khudiram, Prafulla Chaki, Satyen Bose and Kanailal; in July 1909, Cama and Shyamaji demanded a memorial monument at London to pay tribute to their patriotic zeal.

Madam Bhikhaji Cama

Educated at the universities of Madras and Calcutta, a close friend of the cousins of Sri Aurobindo, Chatto left for Paris in 1909 to help Cama edit her paper. Dogged by British police agents he fled to Germany in April 1914, joining the University of Halle for a PhD in philosophy. There he was warmly greeted by his admirer Avinash Bhattacharya or "Bhatta" (1885-1967), PhD in Science and research fellow at the Institute of Chemistry, frequenting the very high society members. In addition to his scientific works, Bhatta regularly contributed articles

Virendranath Chattopadhyay ("Chatto")

* The year of Virendranath Chattopadhyay's death is not certain.

** The year of Raoji Rana's death is not known.

on Indian culture to the first grade German press, much appreciated by the elite. In collaboration with Baron von Bertheim of the Foreign Office and Baron Max Freiher von Oppenheim (1860-1946), officer specialist of Middle East, Chatto created the Berlin Committee ("Deutscher Verein der Freunde Indien") under the presidency of Albert Ballin (1857-1918), Director of the Hamburg-Amerika Steamer Company—it counted among its members patriots from all over Germany and Switzerland. They represented various social and religious origins from all over India:

(1) Dada Chanji Kersasp, close friend of Dhiren (brother of Professor Benoy Sarkar), coming from the USA (University of Iowa) for higher studies in Berlin. Thanks to Gadhar revolutionaries like Taraknath Das, G.D. Kumar and Professor Surendra Mohan Bose, at San Francisco he had been trained in manufacturing and handling all sorts of explosives. (2) Sambhushiva Rao of Madras, brought up at Calcutta to become a Brahmo missionary, had spent years in Austria and Hungary. (3) Dr. Joshi, (4) Gopal Paranjape, (5) Vishnu Suktankar, (6) Abdul Hafiz (PhD in philosophy from the University of Leipzig), (7) Raghunath Panduranga Karandikar emissary of B.G. Tilak and former resident of India House at London), (8) Moresvar Govindrao Prabhakar (Professor of Chemistry at the University of Cologne), (9) Satish Ray, (10) Narainswami Marathe, (11) Dr. Jnan Dasgupta (Chemist appointed by Hoffman-Laroche at Basle), (12) Shrish Chandra Sen (Professor of Sanskrit and Philosophy, Bagha Jatin's emissary), (13) Abder Rahman (University of Freiburg), (14) Siddiqi (University of Gottingen, hailing from Hyderabad, like Chatto, with a scholarship), and (15) Mansur Ahmed (PhD student in Arabic philology).

On 30 September 1914, in the presence of von Oppenheim, of Albert Ballin and of the minister Clementz von Delbruk (1856-1921), Prince Heinz, the Kaiser's brother, received Chatto and Bhatta and gave them the solemn assurance of the Government of Germany in favour of a contract immediately valid in fourteen clauses including "does not call for any intervention of the German army" and—three years before the Bolshevik revolution in Russia—with "the desire of establishing a Socialist Republic in India."[86] Known as the Zimmermann Plan, the points of the contract included:

(1) For generating and guiding revolution in India, we require money, arms and, if necessary, some expert army officers.
(2) For consolidating revolt, the German government should immediately arrange to send some of our colleagues to India.
(3) Train young Indians at Spandau or in some other military explosives factory.
(4) Other young men to be trained in marine factories like Kiel, Bremen, Lubeck for manufacture and use of sea-mines.
5) To write, print and distribute subversive literature in Indian languages under the care of specialised German establishments.
6) To make available to the Indian revolutionary committee some air planes useful for this propaganda.
7) To deliver rapidly materials and military facilities on Indian ports.
8) To issue banknotes of 10 rupees denomination for the use of the secret preparations in India.
9) To endow the Indian revolutionary committee, installed in Berlin, of all possibility to guide revolutionary work in India.
10) In case of a successful revolution, we shall establish our own Socialist Republic of India,[87] without any Austro-German intervention.
11) To make no concession to the Indian Principalities susceptible to oppose this plan.
12) To grant necessary protection to Indian revolutionaries that would ask political asylum in Germany in case the operation fails.
13) Contrary to the antecedent of the Savarkar case, Germany

would not yield to any pressure of the Allies asking to expel anybody belonging to this revolutionary effort in India.

14) Same precaution will be valid for the families or the children of the revolutionaries who would need the protection of the Kaiser's government.[88]

Historian Arun Chandra Guha admires, pertinently, in this contract, the explicit precaution of the Indian revolutionaries not to call on armed intervention from Germany and he observes that this desire to found a Socialist Republic in India preceded by three years the Bolshevik Revolution in Russia.[89]

By the end of September 1914, in two separate lots, Dr. Joshi, Professor Shrish Sen, Rao, Bhatta and Satish Ray—in the company of other members—left Berlin to meet the Jugantar leaders at Calcutta. They insisted on the urgent need of consolidating the revolutionary links at Batavia where representatives of the German government would wait for them. At the same time, Marathe and Dhiren Sarkar, two delegates of the Berlin Committee left for Washington DC to meet the German Ambassador Heinrich von Bernstorff (1862-1939) with coded instructions of the Foreign Office stitched under the lining of their coats. Bernstorff, accordingly commissioned von Papen (1879-1969), his military attaché to purchase adequate quantity of arms and ammunition to be shipped from the coast of California to ports in the Bay of Bengal, via Batavia. Official messages from New York, dated 7 December 1914, 11 February and 27 March 1915 confirm von Papen's stocking on board the schooner *Annie Larsen* 11,000 guns, 250 Mauser revolvers with sufficient ammunition, to be loaded in the 200 tons cargo steamer *Maverick* and delivered to Indian ports.[90]

Leaving Washington DC, Sarkar and Marathe met at San Francisco, Taraknath Das, Herambalal Gupta and other leaders who had been looking after the Gadhar since Har Dayal's hurried departure for Geneva. Several of them, in response to

Taraknath Das

Chatto's call, followed Barakatullah. Raja Mahendra Pratap (1886-1979), decorated by the Kaiser and carrying credentials from him, set out for Kabul, on 10 April 1915, on mission in the company of Otto von Hentig (1886-1984). Led by Oskar Ritter von Niedermayer (1885-1948), a second mission joined them. They raised an army of liberation with Indian soldiers from various British regiments imprisoned by the Germans. Their object was to storm into India from the Afghan front.

Indian Revolutionaries in the USA

Bagha Jatin's emissary, Taraknath Das (1884-1958) had joined the University of California, Berkeley, in 1907. At the same time, he established with friends the Indian Independence League to bring together Indian immigrants, to give them an exact idea of their rights on the spot and their duties towards India, often helping them as intermediary between them and the American authorities. He took the competitive examination for U.S. civil admission to be employed as an interpreter by the Immigration Office at Vancouver. Having launched his paper *Free Hindustan* in October 1907, he invited his former colleague Guran Ditt Kumar—hailing from Bannu, NWFP—to run the *Swadesh Sevak*, a Gurumukhi edition of his paper. Protesting against all injustice imposed by the British regime at Vancouver, in January 1908, Tarak opened an evening school for the "Hindu" immigrants. Turned into the father of the political conscience of his compatriots, Tarak was dismissed from his job and had to shift his journal to Seattle. Henceforth, giving free expression to his convictions, he drew the attention of George Freeman, the Irish revolutionary, editor of the *Gaelic American* who invited him to share with him his New York office from August 1908.

Meticulously following the instructions of Bagha Jatin, thanks to his brilliant university career Tarak was admitted to the most coveted University of Norwich in Vermont for advanced military training. As a logical result of this training, whereas he had applied for joining the Vermont National Guard in June 1909, under pressure from the British authorities, the University put an end to his enrolment. Under a similar pressure, in November 1910, Freeman had to stop publishing Tarak's journal. In 1911, Tarak founded the East India Federation, counting on the participation of numerous Indian associations thriving in the USA and Canada. This was the prototype of the powerful Federation that was to be called Gadhar directed by Har Dayal. Simultaneously, Tarak could undertake his PhD thesis in political science and international relationship—after a prestigious viva voce, it was to receive congratulations from specialists all over the world. Expecting to get rid of the dogging British Police, in 1914 he became a citizen of the USA. Relentless fighter till the end of his life, Tarak was to continue teaching political science at the universities of Columbia and Georgetown.

The Foreign Office at London had intensified its Intelligence investigation in the USA and Canada hoping to curb the nefarious activities of the Indian rcvolutionaries flourishing in North America. Among them top most names were: Taraknath Das, G.D. Kumar, Maulana Barakatullah (1864-1928), Harnam Singh "Sahri", Surendramohan Bose. Thus the US engagement in favour of the British was to modify the situation considerably. Since 1907, Barakatullah had been receiving regularly at his New York apartment, visits of Samuel L. Joshi and Freeman. Six years later, Barakatullah left for Tokyo to teach Hindustani at the university.

With the expansion of the Gadhar base, in May 1913, Kumar left San Francisco for establishing a basis at Manila in the Philippine Islands. He wanted this to act as a forwarding depot which can supervise the work near China, Hong Kong and Shanghai. He continued to remain in touch with Bhagwan Singh and Professor Barakatullah in Japan. He collected funds for the Gadhar, remitting them to Har Dayal. Later, at Yokohama, he was to look after the Gadhar militants returning to India.[91]

The last time we hear about Kumar—the dedicated soul—was at the trial of the *Hindu German Conspiracy* 1917-18 at San Francisco, when Taraknath Das took a leading part in defence of his compatriots, according to the special list in the Record Group 118 and a cutting of the *San Francisco Chronicle* dated 19 January 1918 (Archives of the U.S. Attorney).

One year after his reaching Japan, inspired by a Pan Islamic alliance, as an honest *Musalman* and Indian patriot, Barakatullah published his journal, the "Islamic Fraternity". Moving across Constantinople, Cairo and Petrograd, he resumed contact with friends at the India House, London, before returning to Tokyo. From January 1912, he started condemning the predatory instinct of the English. In 1913, dismissed from his job, just before the declaration of the World War, Barakatullah returned to San Francisco to assist Tarak Das.

The Insurrection

The massive exodus of the Gadhar members from the USA toward Punjab consolidated this enthusiasm. Often reaching Calcutta (like the *Komagata Maru*), they were welcomed mainly by Atulkrishna Ghose and Satish Chakravarti, representing Bagha Jatin. As such, in November 1914, Bagha Jatin received the visit of Kartar Singh Sarabha (1896-1915),

Vishnu Pingley

Kartar Singh Sarabha

and Pingley in the company of his emissary Satyen Sen of the Ghadar (all the three returning with fresh news from Berlin). In 1906, after a closeted meeting with Bagha Jatin—one by one—Taraknath Das, Satyen, his cousin Shrish Sen, and Adhar Laskar had left India.

Kartar Singh Sarabha (1896-1915) was sixteen when he had joined the University of California, Berkeley for studying chemistry. Thanks to his intimacy with Indian revolutionaries like Bhai Paramanand and Taraknath, he discovered how blatant was the discrimination against coloured people. Roused by Har Dayal's call, in 1913, he gave up his studies to look after the Gurumukhi edition of the *Gadhar* ("The Revolt") and composing patriotic songs. He accompanied Satyen and Pingley first of all to keep Bagha Jatin abreast of the developments under the Zimmermann Plan; then, to receive at Calcutta and expedite to the North the hundreds of Gadhar militants assembled to participate in the uprising led by Bagha Jatin and Rash Behari Bose. As for Vishnu Ganesh Pingley (?[*]-1915), a student at the University of California, Berkeley, who hailed from a Brahmin family at Pune and was a friend of Kartar, he too played an important role in the leadership of the Gadhar. On their way home, the three met Dr. Sun Yat Sen (1866-1925) who expressed his will to help them.

Kartar and Pingley went to Benares in November 1914, carrying instructions from Bagha Jatin for Bose. Henceforth, in consultation with Bagha Jatin—who arranged to visit Benares in January 1915—Rash Behari Bose with a team of Bengali experts installed two factories for making explosives, one in Amritsar, the other in Lahore. Having strategically preferred the imminent arrival of German arms before an uprising,

* The year of Vishnu Ganesh Pingley's birth is not known.

Bagha Jatin agreed, however, to Rash Behari's desiring of using the availability of the Sikh repatriates who had joined hands with indoctrinated soldiers from different regiments inside India and with batches of students, all impatient to overthrow British oppression. They fixed 21 February 1915 for the first nation-wide uprising spreading simultaneously from Lahore to Calcutta, passing by Jabalpur and Benares. "Bombs were prepared; arms were got together; flags were made ready; a declaration of war was drawn up; instruments were collected for destroying railways and telegraph wires. In the meantime, however, in order to raise funds for the financing of the enterprise, some Punjab revolutionaries had committed various dacoities."[92] The likeness of style—already in force in Calcutta, as part of Bagha Jatin's programme—led further to the discovery of the types of Bengali bombs, declared the Rowlatt Report.

Dogged by Spies

Unfortunately, among the repatriated Sikhs, there was one Kripal Singh[93], a spy who had been trained by the notorious Hopkinson[94] in USA and mandated by him. Making use of the influence of his cousin Balwant Singh (an indoctrinated officer of the 2nd Cavalry), Kripal had been in the know of the decisions which he transmitted promptly to the Police.[95] Warned soon about the role of this spy, on 16 February, the revolutionaries advanced the date of insurrection by two days; but it could only sow confusion in the extended chain of patriots, with so little training. Pingley and Rash Behari. dispersed before a general search in the districts, revealed the existence of weapons, of bomb components and four national flags. During massive arrests, Pingley was incarcerated in the night of 23 March, in possession of ten bombs, along with sympathisers who had sheltered him in the barrack of the 12th Cavalry in Meerut; among them, Nadir Khan (an Afghan officer, whom Pingley had presented to Rash Behari) turned into informer for the Police.

Let us keep in mind a few points. Sir Michael O'Dwyer, Police representative responsible for the supervision of Ludhiana and specialised in the supervision of the activities of the eight thousand repatriated Gadhar members, had the impression that the British government in India sat on "a snarling volcano".[96] Having alerted the authorities, since December 1914, and urgently renewing his demands in February and in March 1915, to remedy this inadmissible state of things, he finally obtained, in March 1915, the enforcement of the aforementioned Defence of India Act—it allowed leaving aside the established procedures and to detain without trial all seditious suspects as long as "necessary". A vast campaign ensued against the patriots and they were arrested by the hundreds or assigned to home internment. Pingley, Kartar Singh and five other main personalities were awarded capital punishment. In spite of precautions taken by the Police, Kripal Singh was assassinated.

The Second Front of Betrayal

During Tarak's academic mission in the far east, Godfrey Charles Denham of Central Intelligence Department, British India, on 18 March 1917, searched without warrant his apartment at 44 Portola Street, San Francisco and confiscated his papers and books, though Tarak was a U.S. citizen since 1914. Leaked out in the Press, the news roused American public opinion against the pro-English policy of President Wilson. Truly speaking, Wilson's admiration for the English people and a certain disdain for the coloured people—even if they were U.S. citizens—created a climate of diffidence towards these brown-skinned immigrants from Asia challenging the well-being of the English colonial system. Picked up from the secret military service, William Wiseman and Norman Thwaits sent to Washington one "Robertson" (a pseudonym) as an agent at the Department of Justice. At the same time they recruited a batch of refugees from Central Europe to keep a watch on the shipment of smuggled materials to be delivered in Germany.

In 1915, Emmanuel Victor Voska (1875-1960), double

agent appointed by Tomás Garrigue Masaryk (1850-1957), the future president of Czechoslovakia, had brought together into a network his compatriots, a minority in the USA, putting up to date their spying activity on the German and Austrian diplomats who were hostile to the interests of USA and its allies. W.C. Hopkinson, born in Delhi, son of an English sergeant, fluent in several languages of the North, was commissioned by the Indian Colonial Police to supervise the causal link between the revolutionary agitations inside India and the unrest in Canada and North America. He was more directly paid to dog Tarak since his reaching USA via Canada. Hopkins recruited the zealous Kripal Singh to remain further abreast of the Gadhar militants' doings. He also sensed that the erstwhile Jugantar militant Chandra Kanta Chakravarty was of a particular interest.

Earning the confidence of the Berlin Committee, Chandra had been replacing Herambalal Gupta, as link between Berlin Committee and the Ghadar via Embassy of Germany in Washington DC. Initiated as a pious Brahmachari by Swami Abhedananda at the Vedanta Centre of New York, Chandra had rented the basement of the same building (at 494, East 141st Street) and shared it with his German accomplice Ernst Sekunna, a pawn-broker. Trying to rent a room for himself, Hopkinson discovered that Sekunna was the real proprietor of the building. The housekeeper, a Czech refugee belonging to Voska's circle, disclosed that lots of Indians from India, England, France and Germany had been frequenting the basement and he found there "doubtful literature and newspapers from all over the world," negligently scattered all over. The Czech housekeeper had been recording Hopkinson's visits, too.

Sekunna had been running a bogus enterprise first of all to divert German funds to a flourishing bank account, to purchase real estates at New York and, also, on the other hand, to continue his plans as a double agent. Inflated by this success, Chandra ceased to be cautious—having fanned the curiosity of the Czech agents, he left plenty of written proofs of his doings inside their apartment at 364 West 120th Street de New York. Emmanuel Victor Voska and Ladislav Urban rejoiced while discovering them. As it has been mentioned in the biography of Bagha Jatin,[97] in course of an purely American vanity fair, New York and Washington societies had been gradually rivalling San Francisco in importance. Ambitious and cunning Chandra discerned the moment when Franz von Papen, the German military Attache, began handling a fabulous amount of money and deciding in favour of the purchase and shipments of arms for India. Though backed by the Berlin Committee, unknown to all patriotic sentiment, Chandra pushed forward his own plans and proposals before the German legation, supported by his German mentor Sekunna. Sekunna had been, above all, a member of the Bureau called Intelligence for the East (*Nachrichtenstelle für den Orient*), created by the German government on the eve of the First World War for the purpose of encouraging and supporting conspiracy and agitations in British India and their satellites in Persia and Egypt. Under the control of the Ministry of Foreign Affairs, its director was Baron Max von Oppenheim—throughout the War, it was to collaborate intimately with the Khedive Abbas II of Egypt and the Indian revolutionary organisations such as the Berlin Committee, the Jugantar, the Gadhar, along with eminent Muslim socialists like Maulvi Barakatullah. In addition to von Oppenheim, it counted as members Franz von Papen, Gunther von Wesendonck, Wilhelm Wasmus (so-called "Lawrence of Germany"), Ernst Sekunna and others. It was directly in charge of happenings connected with the Indo-German Plot, including affairs like uprisings in Bengal, the Gadhar trips, the requisitioning of the schooner *Annie Larsen*, the raising of an army of liberation on the Thai-Burmese frontier, and other less known events in the Near East and the borders between British India and Afghanistan. It was busy destabilising the British hold on the Muslims in India, Middle East and Egypt. It had the credit of the first conspiracies in Turkey and of the *Jihad* issued by the Caliph. In addition to spying and sending seditious missions to Persia and Afghanistan, the Bureau looked after the recruiting—in collaboration with the Berlin Committee—the Indian soldiers imprisoned by Germany in Mesopotamia.[98]

Thanks to Papen's introduction to the German Ambassador Bernstorff in person, Chandra—increasingly greedy, "described as the oily leader of an oily revolution."[99]—obtained an official post with an amazing salary. In the published reports of the *Hindu German* case, Chandra emerges "as an unscrupulous, deceitful and cowardly figure."[100] A letter from the Home Ministry warned Leeland Harrison against Chandra, not to have enough trust in "our little friend" by giving him the responsibility he hopes to have; he can lie faster than a horse can trot and "he is capable of crawling across a keyhole."[101]

Let us switch back to the house-keeper of the building at San Francisco where Chandra and Sekunna lived. The man came from Moravia and belonged to Voska's faction of Czech revolutionaries. Having had a free access to the apartment of the Indians and their German agents, Voska appointed spies to follow the cue of the Indo-German network up to China. Quite a few of his contacts—apparently Austrian patriots—passed on to the most important facts to Voska by intercepting messages from Von Papen, replies from Zimmermann, detailed information about the dispatch of arms and ammunition on board the *Annie Larsen* and the *Maverick* to be delivered to revolutionaries in India, including plots of sabotage in American explosive factories, etc.[102] On reaching Masaryk in time at London, these details created such an enormous panic in the international exchange of the Allies that—especially after having put an end to the vital delivery of arms thanks to the swift intervention of the British navy—Masaryk received, in return, in addition to due credit and prestige, several well deserved rewards.

Bagha Jatin's Heritage

Voska described several of these characters and events later in his book.[103] These were notes that "referred to not just minor events but to those that had international impact and historic consequences including India's freedom movement," admits Ross Hedvíček, an American publicist of Czech origin. "Yes, perfectly so," confirms Ross, who claims: "Had E.V. Voska not interfered in this history, today nobody would have heard about Mahatma Gandhi and the father of the Indian nation would have been Bagha Jatin."[104] He further notes: "Bagha Jatin wanted to free India from the British hold but he had the idea of allying against them with the Germans from whom he expected to receive arms and other helps. Voska learnt it through his network and, as pro-American, pro-British and anti-German, he spoke of it to T.G. Masaryk." The latter rushed to keep the institutions informed about it.

Thus, Voska transmitted it to Masaryk, Masaryk to the Americans, the Americans to the British. On friendly terms with the Jews of Central Europe, T.G. Masaryk knew how, blackmailed by the Jewish lobby—mainly by Samuel Untermyer of the law firm "Guggenheim, Untermeyer and Marshall"—President Wilson was opposed to the activities of the British Indian immigrants in America. Masaryk mentions most of these facts in the English version of his book. Whereas the Jews had been raising funds for establishing Israel in the Middle East, Indian patriots—as expected by Bernhardi—collaborated with the Pan-Islamist current.[105]

Having perfectly sensed the multiple play of diffidence and duplicity inside the country and abroad, when—in June 1915—Bagha Jatin came to know about the failure of the arms expedition, instead of lamenting over the shattering of so many years of painstaking labour, he is reported to have stated in a calm voice: "God has rectified our decision. We had wished to free India with another foreign power. But India has to rise with her own strength." When as a consolation, some dare-devil associates proposed to carry on other attempts to import arms by land, Bagha Jatin—while going through the ominous newspaper cutting received from Penang—chuckled and said: "Country's salvation from within!"[106] Nalinikanta Kar, present in this closeted meeting, was to write to Bagha

Jatin's grandson that this utterance reminded everybody about the intimate wish of the leader: *amra morbo, jat jagbe!* ("We shall die [so that] the Nation wakes up").

With time, it is recognised that Bagha Jatin with his heroic death, in 1915, did not only inaugurate the second phase of his revolutionary project but, almost simultaneously, by preparing the field for Gandhi's triumphal encounter with Destiny, he initiated even the third phase.

Bhupati Majumdar (1890-1973), one of the followers of Bagha Jatin—who was to occupy several ministerial posts in the Government of West Bengal since India's independence—signed to Bagha Jatin alone the creation of the international revolutionary network, during the First World War, for winning India's freedom.[107] Militant nationalism was no more a dream. The Berlin Committee had started raising an army of liberation with Indian soldiers from various British regiments captured by the Germans in the Middle East, with a view to invade India in a pincers movement: remote controlled from Berlin, in the West, through Afghanistan, under the leadership of Mahendra Pratap. And, from San Francisco, in the East, through Burma, via Thailand, joining the insurrection flaring from the Fort William at Calcutta up to Punjab. Bagha Jatin was fond of saying : "Thailand will be our Switzerland of Asia."

After a meticulous study of the documents concerning the *Howrah* Case and the writings of revolutionaries involved, the critical and prudent look of Amales Tripathi reveals more explicitly "the new and original currents" released by Jatin Mukherjee's policy:

(a) to forge a revolutionary consciousness with the help of sporadic but daring acts and individual martyrdom;

(b) to organise an armed resistance in small groups, concomitant with an effort to improve the general (particularly financial) level of the people's life;

(c) to requisition arms, from native sources (like the *Rodda* case) and by importing them (with German collaboration via Californian coast);

(d) to strengthen a guerilla organisation;

(e) to indoctrinate native soldiers in different regiments (such as the 10th Jats and the 16th Rajput Rifles) and to launch an all-Indian uprising.[108]

Just as we have come across two opposite trends active in the freedom movement—Moderate and Extremist—it will be necessary for us also to become aware of the two contradictory factions within this last one: (a) members of the Anushilan, reactionary, centralised, based in Dhaka and more active in East Bengal; (b) those of the Jugantar, progressive, decentralised, mainly active in North and West Bengal, and Upper India. With the advent of Gandhi, the Jugantar was to learn to appraise the direction taken by the much awaited popular revolution and was to side with Gandhi up to the limit of its compatibility and their convictions; the others—along with Indian Communists—were to oppose him up to the point of collaborating with the colonial policy. Since the opening chapter of his autobiography, Pratul Ganguli, one of the main leaders of the Anushilan, gives vent to an apology of his belonging to *brahman* orthodoxy and, as grist to his mill, he puts some words in Bagha Jatin's mouth claiming him also as a champion of this superiority by birth.

Such a vain and false enterprise is regretted by all lovers of history, because Bagha Jatin's entire life and whatever he taught were but a long and solid protest against discriminations and superstitions of all kind, welling from hazards of birth, against fatalism, against idle speculations, against social and economic sectarianism, against the humiliation and the injustice of men that put down men, notably in the colonial context. It will be seen, how, since his teenage, Jatin participated in hand to hand tournaments between opponents who were both 'touchables' and 'untouchables'. During the annual religious festivities, Jatin was seen imploring his uncle to put an end to social favouritism wherein quality rice was served to men of upper castes and a coarse variety to the others. He shared the earthen platter with an old Muslim lady. In 1905, during the agitations against the Partition of Bengal, Jatin was to seat side by side militants—

Muslims and Hindus of all classes—around communal meals, to affirm the fraternity between Indians. He welcomed all his brothers—disciples and political associates—from all social levels and put them up as his household members.[109] One of his childhood friends and revolutionary colleagues, Kunjalal Saha, hailed from a lower caste. Another, Bhavabhushan Mitra—belonging to the caste of kayastha[110]—was fond of informing Jatin's grandchildren: "During his emergency missions, often I had the chance of accompanying him. I remember that epoch when it was difficult to find volunteers to cremate dead bodies belonging to the lower caste citizens, or victims of tuberculosis or contagious epidemics; all infringement to these social inhibitions was liable to ostracism. Jatin took a particular pleasure in organising such ceremonies overtly." Among other "new and original currents that were released by Jatin Mukherjee", Bhavabhushan was amused to underline in utter lucidity: "We, who had no right to wear the sacred thread of *upavita*, under his influence, we wore it and we practised the rituals reserved to the *brahmans*, whereas many others (like himself) who had had it by their birth, discarded it merrily." Since his childhood, Jatin's innate humanitarian devotion had been fed by the teaching and the uncompromising example his own mother Sharat Shashi Devi, even before his meeting with Swami Vivekananda.

While waiting for the consignments of arms, on the East coast of the Indian peninsula in Bengal and in Orissa, the supreme choice that presented itself to Bagha Jatin and his four associates, on 9 September 1915 was whether to flee the approaching armed Police (a flight which was amply possible thanks to their topographic knowledge of the region and the administrative facilities of international travel), or to sacrifice their life in a pitched resistance. They adopted the second solution of courting death to liberate the minds of people enslaved by multiple fears: fear to live, fear to disobey, fear to die. These five revolutionaries wanted to leave before their companions in arms an unforgettable model of selfless patriotism, strategy and heroism. On the morning of 10 September 1915, Charles Tegart, Deputy Commissioner of the British Indian Police (Calcutta), went to Jatin Mukherjee's bedside during his last hours at the Balasore hospital. It is learnt that among the Tegart Papers, preserved in the South Asian Study Centre Archives, University of Cambridge, there is a work entitled, *Revolutionaries of Bengal* by Hemanta Kumar Sarkar, published in 1923 by Indian Book Club. The author has recorded Tegart's reply to the Barrister J.N. Ray's enquiry about the rumours concerning Jatin Mukherjee's death, shortly after the Battle of Balasore (pp.56): "Unfortunately he is dead." Ray remarked, "Why unfortunately?" Tegart is reported to have acknowledged: "Though I had to do my duty, I have a great admiration for him. He was the only Bengali who died in an open fight from a trench." In the margin of this passage there is a check mark, presumably by Tegart himself, attesting the accuracy of this statement.[111]

It is worth noticing that later, in agreement with the usual tone employed by Western observers such as Chirol, Ker, Rowlatt, upto Judith Brown, Tegart was to write: "In the character of Jatin (...) and most of the other enthusiasts, the visionary was stronger than the realist (...)" Tegart added to this tribute: "At the same time, their driving power was immense." Let us not forget that such praise was rather rare from the English administrators. Talking about Gandhi and Nehru, L.S Amery (Minister for Indian Affairs) found them "niggling unpractical creatures",[112] while Linlithgo regretted, "They could never run straight." Setting apart the average condescending assessment of the natives, Tegart was further eloquent when he admitted, nevertheless, that if—according to Jatin Mukherjee's project—the army of liberation composed of ten thousand patriots could have received an adequate training in the Thai-Burmese frontier, and if the consigned ships could deliver the weapons and the munitions in an Indian port, the British would lose the First World War.[113]

People often speculate on the nature of the government that the Indian patriots would have choosen, had the Zimmerman Plan not failed. We think, first of all, it would have been secular, composed of really Pan-Indian members. Both internal evidences of the so-called extremist—radical—Jugantar party inside India, and the working abroad of the Gadhar in the United States and the Berlin Committee in Europe leave us an ample hope that, first of all, deserving and competent leaders from all the communities: Hindu (e.g. Taraknath Das, Lala Har Dayal, Chatto or Viren Chattopadhyaya), Muslim (e.g. Maulana Barakatullah, Obeidullah Sindhi), Parsi (Dada Chanji Kersasp) and Sikh (e.g. Bhagwan Singh) would get their chance to collaborate harmoniously, with authority and conviction. Slowly, the ever-alert eyes of Hopkinson detected within the fold of the Gadhar, however, a pro-Sikh trend of separatism creeping in. It was another Sikh who chose mercilessly to put an end to the long persecution of this evil-doer in October 1914.

While Bagha Jatin and Rash Behari Bose had been preparing the insurrection inside India, on 12 February 1915, Chatto presented Raja Mahendra Pratap to the Kaiser with the proposal of leading a delegation to Kabul and marching into British Indian territory. Sensing a possible betrayal and considering failures to be pillars of success, Bagha Jatin had chalked out a series of overt actions preceding and following the 21 February insurrection, both for supplying funds as well as for bucking up the militants' spirits. On 12 February, a spectacular taxi-cab hold-up at Garden Reach yielded a haul of Rs. 18,000 (a fabulous sum). As I have described elsewhere[114], this "new feature in revolutionary crime" (to quote the Rowlatt) had just been introduced in France by the gang of the anarchist Jules Joseph Bonnot (1876-1912). On 22 February, the Beliaghata dacoity brought a booty of Rs. 22,000. On 24 February, while holding a secret meeting on Pathguriaghata Street, a stranger entered the apartment and called out Bagha Jatin's name. Shot at and taken to be dead, the spy mentioned Bagha Jatin in his dying declaration. On the 28th, near Hedua, a blacklisted Bengali police inspector was shot dead. As a response to Bagha Jatin's reign of terror, emergency measures were introduced—armoured cars, flying squads, drop-gates, sirens, patrolling of armed sentries, placards announcing a fat reward—Jatin Mukherjee wanted, dead or alive![115] Pingley was arrested on 23 March and hanged. Pursued by a warrant, Rash Behari left for Japan on 12 May 1915, with the hope of continuing his revolutionary activities abroad.

The mission under Pratap and von Hentig left Berlin on 10 April 1915. Not yet informed about the failure of the arms expedition and the self-giving of Bagha Jatin on 9 September, they reached Kabul on 2 October 1915. Two months later, Pratap formed there a temporary Government of Free India under his presidency, with Barakatullah as the Prime Minister and Obeidullah Sindhi as Home Minister. Had Bagha Jatin been living, he would have—as usual—chosen to act from behind the stage and would have invited to this cabinet some of the seasoned associates like Rash Behari Bose, Viren Chattopadhyay, Bhupendranath Datta and his loyal followers like Taraknath Das, Naren Bhattacharya (M.N. Roy), Atulkrishna Ghose, for various portfolios. Knowing Sri Aurobindo's reticence to leave Pondicherry, he would have invited Tilak as the first president of Free India. And, probably as Prime Minister, an apparent outsider—Muhammad Ali Jinnah (1976-1948).

Before the stepping in of Gandhiji (and Jawaharlal Nehru, his follower), Jinnah had been known for his ardent patriotic profile, eager to serve India most sincerely; a follower of Dadabhai Naoroji, he had been well off with three major trends of the Congress: (a) Pheroze Shah Mehta (the Liberal); (b) Gopal Krishna Gokhale (the Moderate); (c) Bal Gangadhar Tilak (the Radical). He had been working hard to incite the reticent Muslims to join active politics in a climate of Hindu-Muslim fraternity. Out of a personal instinctive dislike for Jinnah, Gandhi as well as Nehru had failed to appreciate his genuinely centripetal contribution. Can any student of history ever forget Subhas Chandra Bose who, in 1939, had been re-elected President of the National Congress for the second time, but had to resign under the manipulative machinations of the Mahatma? Similarly, had Jinnah not been victim of this chronic misunderstanding, had he not been systematically looked down upon, there would have been no Khilafat, no exploitation by agent provocateurs (like the Ali brothers); paramount in a series of no-this and no-that there would have been no heinous communal riots in 1946 under the Muslim League ruling, no tragic Noakhali, no Partition, no genocide, even no Pakistan at all.

People ask whether Gandhiji ever mentioned Bagha Jatin's contribution in the history of India's freedom movement. It is known that with Sri Aurobindo's approval, in 1920, the former Jugantar militants—all of them, followers of Bagha Jatin (like Jadugopal Mukherjee, Bhupendrakumar Datta, Arunchandra Guha, Surendramohan Ghose)—espoused non-violence as a policy on condition of resuming their own method whenever needed, to rectify Gandhiji's failure, as in 1923. The Mahatma, more than once, expressed his appreciation of the quality of collaboration he received from them. But in spite of Deshabandhu Chittaranjan's public tribute saluting the memory of Gopinath Saha as a martyr, in 1924, when Gandhiji was requested to confirm this homage from the Congress platform, he refused. Seven years later, the same Gandhiji, under pressure, agreed to honour the self-giving of Bhagat Singh, hanged under similar circumstances as Gopinath.

In August 1947, I had the fortune of spending a day in Gandhiji's company. All my attitude of hero worship vanished when I was informed that the Mahatma was to leave Calcutta in a hurry in order to avoid witnessing the first country-wide celebration of Bagha Jatin's glorious death in independent India on 9 September 1947.

In a recent revelation we come across information that in 1925, however, Gandhiji is reported to have told Tegart that Jatin Mukherjee, generally referred to as "Bagha Jatin", was "a divine personality". Little did he know that Tegart had once mentioned to his colleagues that if Jatin were an Englishman, the English people would have built his statue next to Nelson's at Trafalgar Square. In his note to J. E. Francis of the India Office in 1926, Tegart described Bengali revolutionaries as "the most selfless political workers in India".[116]

Notes

1. Bhupendranath Datta (Vivekananda's yougest brother), *Swami Vivekananda*, Navabharat Publishers, Calcutta, 1986 (2nd Edition), 162 (Swami).
2. (Swami), 163.
3. *Les racines intellectuelles du mouvement d'indépendance de l'Inde (1893-1918)*, by Prithwindra Mukherjee, Editions Codex, 2010, 121. Also cf: *The Dedicated*, by Lizelle Reymond, J. Day & Co, New York, 1953, 222.
4. Quoted by Bhupendranath Datta, in *Bharater Dvitiya Svadhinata Samgram*, Navabharat, Calcutta, 1949 (BND), 99.
5. (BND), 2.
6. *Prophets of the New India*, A. & C. Boni, New York, 1930, 497
7. Margaret Noble (1857-1911), Vivekananda's Irish disciple, intimately engaged in India's freedom fight.
8. K.R. Srinivasa Iyengar, *Sri Aurobindo: A Biography and A History*, Sri Aurobindo International Centre of Education, Pondicherry, Vol.1, March 1972 (3rd revised and enlarged edition), (Iyengar), 594.
9. *Les racines intellectuelles du mouvement d'indépendance de l'Inde (1893-1918)*, Prithwindra Mukherjee, Editions Codex, 2010.
10. cf: Relevant article in the present anthology.
11. "Prabandha-pustak" (1879) in *Bankim-rachanavali*, Sahitya Samsad, Vol. II, 1973, 213.
12. *Navayug'er Bangala*, Bipinchandra Pal, 1964, 133 (Pal).
13. (Pal), 135.
14. (Swami), 107.
15. (RNT), 424-5.
16. (Swami), 08.

17. *Swami Vivekanand'er vani o rachana*, Udbodhan Office, Calcutta, Vol. II, 122.
18. *The Complete Works of Swami Vivekananda*, Advaita Ashram, Almora, 1937 (CWSV) Vol. IV, 313.
19. Ibid., 406-7.
20. This appeal by Vivekananda was first published in his Bengali review *Udbodhan*, later included in CWSV.
21. "My Plan of Campaign" in CWSV/III, 216.
22. BM/MNI, 25.
23. "The Future of India" in CWSV/III, 301-302.
24. CWSV/III, 158.
25. "Prachya o paschatya" in (Vvv), 266.
26. *Sri Aurobindo o bangalay svadeshi yug*, Girijashankar Raychaudhuri, Navabharat, Calcutta, 1956, 226.
27. People of low origin, untouchable, often employed for cremating dead bodies.
28. CWSV/VII, 180.
29. CWSV/III, 225.
30. Swami Vivekananda, *Les yogas pratiques*, translated into French by Jean Herbert, Albin Michel, Paris, 1970, 34.
31. CWSV/ III, 296.
32. op. cit., 245.
33. CWSV/IV, 317
34. Unpublished translation by Prithwindra Mukherjee.
35. CWSV, V/152-153. It is interesting to compare such passages directly with Poems 107 and 108 in the English *Gitanjali*, by Rabindranath Tagore.
36. Complete Works of Sri Aurobindo, Birth Centenary Collection, Pondicherry, 1972, Vol. I, 44.
37. CWSV, IV/401.
38. CWSV, VI/375-376.
39. Benoy Kumar Sarkar, foreword to *The Social Philosophy of Vivekananda* by Trilochan Das, Cooperative Book Depot, Calcutta, 1949.
40. *Undying Courage*, Prithwindra Mukherjee, 19.
41. «Swamiji–Nivedita–Jatin Mukherjee» by Prithwindra Mukherjee in Shankariprasad Basu and Sunilbihari Ghose (ed.), *Bhagini Nivedita janma-shatavarshiki smarak grantha*, (BNJS), Vol. II, 5-17; cf: Shankariprasad Basu, *Vivekananda o samakaalin bhaaratvarsha*, (SPB), Vol. VI, 147-149.
42. Translated from the French quoted by Prithwindra Mukherjee, *Les racines intellectuelles*, 97.

43. Nixon's Report in *Terrorism in Bengal* (TIB), Volume II, 509.
44. *Loc. cit.*
45. *Bengalee*, Calcutta 24 March 1912, reproduced by SB/NL, vol. II, 8.
46. *Desh*, Calcutta, 10 July 1982, 23, reproduced in Shankariprasad Basu, *Lokamata Nivedita*, vol. II, 114.
47. Datta Bhupendranath, *Swami Vivekananda, Patriot and Prophet*, Navabharat Publishers, Calcutta, 1954, 8.
48. Based on a chapter of the PhD thesis by Prithwindra Mukherjee, *Les racines intellectuelles du mouvement d'indépendancede l'Inde (1893-1918)*, éditions Codex, 2010.
49. Praelector of King's College and Sri Aurobindo's advisor, G.W. Prothero wrote to James Cotton, admiring the young student's « courage and perseverence », adding that he had « not only ability but character. (cf: Prithwindra Mukherjee, *Sri Aurobindo*, 25; A.B.Purani, *Life of Sri Aurobindo*, 1978 (4th revised ed.), 328.
50. SA/BCL, Vol. 26, *On Himself.*
51. Nevinson's impressions were published in two of his books : *The New Spirit in India* (London, 1909, reprinted by Metropolitan Book Co, Delhi, 1975) and *Fire of Life*, London, 1935. Various passages of this interview appear in the chapters and books on Aurobindo's political activities.
52. Cf : M.N. Roy's article on Jatin Mukherjee (Annexe) and several references in *Terrorism in Bengal.*
53. *L'Évangile universel*, by Romain Rolland, Stock, 1930, pp189-194. Rolland completes the significance of this statement by quoting Sri Aurobindo's translation of the Vedic description of Usha, the Dawn eternal from Kutsa Angirasa in his *Life Divine*, published in the first issue of the French edition of the *Arya*, 15 August 1914.
54. *Prabasi*, Calcutta, July 1928; cf: *Sri Aurobindo: biographie*, by P. Mukherjee, p134; *Resurgent India*, by Sisirkumar Mitra, 389.
55. *Raja Rammohun Roy*, by Saumyendranath Tagore, 44-45; cf: Prithwindra Mukherjee's review of *Rammohun Roy and the Making of Victorian Britain,* by Lynn Zastoupil, Published in 2010 by Palgrave , Macmillan, New York (USA) and Houndmills, Hampshire (UK) in *Journal of the Royal Asiatic Society*, Cambridge University Press, Third Series, Volume 24, Part 3, April 2014.
56. (PAL), 160.
57. *Yogendranath Vidyabhushan*, by Niren Banerjee, Atama Prakashan, 1977, 24.

58. *Parivarik katha*, by Lalitkumar Chatterjee, Sarasvati Press, Krishnagar, 1947, 77.
59. "Swamiji-Nivedita-Jatin Mukherjee" by Prithwindra Mukherjee, in (BNJS), Part II, 1968, 6.
60. "swaraj'er tirtha-path'e nihsanga pathik bipinchandra pal" by Pabitrakumar Gupta, serialised in monthly *Jayashri*, Volume 72, Number 3, July 2007.
61. *Terrorism in Bengal*, compiled by Amiya K. Samanta, Government of West Bengal, 1995, (TIB), Vol. II, 393.
62. *Biplabi jiban'er smriti*, jadugopal mukhopadhyay, 1956, Calcutta, 411.
63. *Biplab'er padachinha*, by Bhupendrakumar Datta, 1973, Calcutta (2nd edition), 222.
64. *Rabindra-rachanabali*, Visvabharati, 2000, (RNT), Vol. 17, 378
65. (RNT), op. cit., 422-3.
66. *New India*, 12 May 1903.
67. Letters of Morley to Minto, Vol. I (d/ 11May 1906), Vol. II (d/ 28 August 1907; 5 December 1907) in M.N. Das, *India under Morley &Minto*, Allen & Unwin, London, 1964.
68. *Political Trouble in India. A Confidential Report*, by James Campbell Ker, Superintendent Government Printing, Calcutta, 1917; Oriental Publication, New Delhi, 1973, 9-10.
69. Iyengar, Vol. I, 594.
70. Iyengar, Vol. II, 684.
71. (Swami), *op. cit.*, 88.
72. Reminiscences by Motilal Roy in *Anandabazar Patrika*, special Jatindra Mukherjee supplement, 9 September, 1947.
73. Sealy's Report in (TIB), Vol. V, 64.
74. Tegart's Report on the Ramakrishna Mission, in (TIB), Vol. IV, 1366.
75. Notes by Nalinikanta Kar, preserved at the Nehru Museum, New Delhi; published in *Bagha Jatin*, by Prithwindra Mukherjee, Dey's Publishing, 1990 (1st Edition), 100.
76. Notes by Manindra Chakravarti, Ibid., published in *Sadhak biplabi Jatindranath*, by Prithwindra Mukherjee, West Bengal State Book Board, 1990, 372-373.
77. (Vvv), 248-9.
78. *The Role of the Gadhar Party in the National Movement*, by Gurdev Singh Deol, Sterling Publishers, Delhi, 1969, 54-55. Consult *Sadhak biplabi Jatindranath*, by Prithwindra Mukherjee, West Bengal State Book Board, 1990, 452 : Chenchia's statement.
79. "Jatindranath Mukherjee" by M.N. Roy, *Independent India*,

February 27, 1949; reprinted in *Men I Met*, Bombay, 1968.

80. Amalendu Dasgupta in *Anandabazar Patrika*, Special Jatin Mukherjee supplement, 9 September, 1947.
81. Revised and enlarged version of an article first published in the internet review of the French Ministry of Foreign Affairs, *Mission Centenaire 1914-1918*, Paris, March 2014.
82. Editorial, *Anandabazar Patrika*, Calcutta du 9 septembre 1927; cf: *Sadhak biplabi Jatindranath* de Prithwindra Mukherjee, West Bengal Book Board, Calcutta (2nd edition, 2012), xxx.
83. «Jatindranath Mukherjee» Editorial de M.N. Roy in *Independent India*, le 27 fevrier 1949; cf: *Les racines intellectuelles du mouvement d'independance de l'Inde (1893-1918)*, de Prithwindra Mukherjee, editions Codex, Talmont StHilaire, 2010, 397.
84. Nalinikanta Kar, quoted in *Bagha Jatin*, by Prithwindra Mukherjee, National Book Trust, New Delhi, 2013 (2nd edition), 99.
85. *Les racines intellectuelles*, de Prithwindra Mukherjee, 191-192.
86. Italics has been added by the author.
87. Abinäsh Bhattacharya, *Europe bharatiya biplab'er sadhana, op. cit.*, 109-110.
88. Dr. Avinash Bhattacharya, *Europe...*, 109-110.
89. Arun Chandra Guha, *First Spark of Revolution,* Orient Longman, New Delhi, 1971, 434.
90. Powerful federation of Indian patriots, based at San Francisco in 1913, out of several associations created by Taraknath Das on the Western coast of North America.
91. Ker, James Campbell, *Political Trouble in India*, 1973, 237, 425.
92. Ibid., 138.
93. "Kirpal Singh was a soldier of the British Indian Army who is best known for his role in passing on to the Punjab CID the intelligence on the date of the Ghadar Conspiracy in February 1915 during World War I. The CID recruited the services of Kirpal Singh in early 1915 following the reports and intelligence it received on the proposed plans for instigating revolt in the British Indian Army in Punjab. Singh, who had a Ghadarite cousin serving in the 23rd Cavalry, was able to infiltrate the leadership, being assigned to work in his cousin's regiment. Singh was soon under suspicion of being a spy, but was able to pass on the information regarding the date and scale of the uprising to British Indian intelligence. As the date for the mutiny approached, a desperate Rash Behari Bose brought forward the D-day to the evening of 19 February, which was discovered by Kirpal Singh on

the very day. No attempts were made by the Ghadarites to restrain him, and he rushed to inform Liaqat Khan of the change of plans. Ordered back to his station to signal when the revolutionaries had assembled, Singh was detained by the would-be mutineers, but managed to make good his escape under the cover of answering the call of nature." (Source: *http://en.wikipedia.org/wiki/Intelligence_Bureau_for_the_East*)

94. «Dr. Taraknath Das (1884-1958)» in *Les racines intellectuelles*, by Prithwindra Mukherjee, 194-202.
95. *Les racines intellectuelles*, 219, 220.
96. *India as I knew it*, by Michael O'Dwyer, Constable, London, 1925, 196-200.
97. Prithwindra Mukherjee, National Book Trust, New Delhi, 2013 (2nd edition).
98. Voska, E.V., Irwin W, *Spy and Counter-spy*, Doubleday, Doran & Co, New York 1940;
(Source: *http://en.wikipedia.org/wiki/Intelligence_Bureau_for_the_East).*
99. Headline of *New York Times*, 10 March 1917, US FederalArchives, Record Group 118, containing declarations by Chakravarti and Sekunna, 6 and 7 March 1917 before the commissioner Seull et al.
100. *In Freedom's Quest*, by Sibnarayan Ray, Minerva Associates, Calcutta, 1998, Vol.I, 71-72, 23.
101. US Federal Archives, Record Group 49, n°845-1.
102. *Spy and Counter-Spy*, by E.V. Voska & W. Irwin, Doubleday, Doran & Co, New York, 1940→London, 1941.
103. Ibid.
104. *CSmagazin*, Srpen 2006. http://www.cs-magazin.com/2006-08/view.php?article=articles/cs0608116.htm. Also *Emigrant, který se vrátil do Česka na důchod* ("The Emigrant Who Returned to Czechia for Retirement").
105. *The Making of a State: Memoirs and Observations, 1914-1918*, London, 1927, 50, 221, 242.
106. Nalinikanta Kar, quoted in *Bagha Jatin*, by Prithwindra Mukherjee, National Book Trust, New Delhi, 2013 (2nd edition), 99.
107. "Dada : Jatindranath Mukherjee" by Bhupati Majumdar, in *Sainik*, Calcutta, 15 August 1948.
108. *Swadhinata samgrame bharater jatiya congress 1885-1947)*, Ananda Publishers, Calcutta, 1991, 77-79.
109. Jatish Pal, who fought by Jatin's side at the Battle of Balasore,

hailed from a marginal family of potters (*chaki*); he had spent several years as one of Jatin's family members, to the point of having being nicknamed by the Hero's three children as Uncle *Chak* ("Wheel").

110. Equivalent to the *kshatriya*, often related to the classes of farmers and warriors, turned into professional scribes.
111. *Terrorism In Bengal*, Vol. III, viii. Hemanta Kumar Sarkar was a native of Krishnagar and had been a class-mate of Netaji Subhas Bose and Bhupendra Kumar Datta for their university studies : all the three in their youth came under the aura of Jatin Mukherjee. Persuaded that the leader of a revolution has to be a *mukta-purusha* ("Liberated Soul"), Subhas asked Bhupen–who had started frequenting Jatin–whether Jatin Mukherjee was a *mukta-purusha*. Confessing his inability to determine the attributes of a *mukta-purusha*, Bhupen could only remark : "All that I know is that Jatin-da fervently lives and practises the teachings of the *Gita*, and knows by heart the entire text." After a night of reflection, Subhas wanted Bhupen to inform Jatin that he was going to follow Jatin's path. This was manifest when during World War II–quite untimely-, Subhas was to take up Jatin's blue print for invading India from the Eastern front.
112. Amery's letter to Linlithgo, dated 2 February, 1942, CM.58; cf Amales Tripathi, *swadhinata samgrame*, 300.
113. Tegart Mss, p128; cf : *op. cit.*, 78.
114. *Bagha Jatin* (NBT), 78-79.
115. Jadugopal Mukhopadhyay, *Biplabi jibaner smriti*, Academic Publishers, Calcutta, 1982 (2nd ed.), 328.
116. "Gandhi, Tegart and the Bengali Terrorist" by Sobhanlal Mukherjee, in the *Statesman*, Calcutta 28 April, 2009, quoted by Prithwindra Mukherjee, in *Bagha Jatin*, National Book Trust, 2013 (2nd edition), 131; cf: Amalendu Dé, "Biplabider sangé mahatma Gandhi o Charles Augustus Tegart Alochana" in *Kalapratima Sahitya Patra*, Vol. 16, septembre 2009, 61-70.

Bibliography

Bandyopadhyay Ashitkumar, Shankariprasad Basu and Shankar editors, *Vishvavivek*, Vak,1963 (Vvv).

Bandyopadhyay Niren, *Yogendranath Vidyabhushan*, Atama Prakashan, Calcutta, 1977, 24.

Basu Shankariprasad and Sunilbihari Ghose (ed.), *Bhagini Nivedita janma-shatavarshiki smarak grantha*, 1968, 2 Vol. (BNJS).

Basu Shankariprasad, *Vivekananda o samakalin bharatvarsha*, Mandal Book House, Calcutta, 1975, 6 Vol.

Basu Shankariprasad, *Lokamata Nivedita*, Ananda Publishers, 1991 (5 volumes).

Chakravarti, Manindra, *Notes* preserved in Jatin Mukherjee Papers, at the Nehru Museum, New Delhi; published in *Sadhak biplabi Jatindranath*, by Prithwindra Mukherjee, West Bengal State Book Board, 1990, 372-373.

Chattopadhyaya, Bankimchandra, "Prabandha-pustak" (1879) in *Bankim-rachanavali*, Sahitya Samsad, Vol. II, 1973.

Chattopadhyay, Lalitkumar, *Parivarik katha*, by, Sarasvati Press, Krishnagar, 1947.

Das M.N., *India under Morley &Minto*, Allen & Unwin, London, 1964.

Dasgupta, Amalendu, "Madaripur'er tin bandhu" in *Anandabazar Patrika*, Special Jatin Mukherjee supplement, 9 September, 1947.

Datta, Bhupendrakumar, *Biplab'er padachinha*, 1973, Calcutta (2nd edition).

Datta, Bhupendranath, *Swami Vivekananda, Patriot and Prophet*, Navabharat Publishers, Calcutta, 1954.

Datta, Bhupendranath, *Swami Vivekananda*, Navabharat Publishers, 1986 (Swami).

Deol, Gurdev Singh, *The Role of the Gadhar Party in the National Movement*, Sterling Publishers, Delhi, 1969.

Gupta, Pabitrakumar, "swaraj'er tirtha-path'e nihsanga pathik bipinchandra pal" serialised in monthly *Jayashri*, Volume 72, Number 3, July 2007.

Iyengar, K.R. Srinivasa, *Sri Aurobindo: a biography and a history*, Sri Aurobindo International Centre of Education, Pondicherry, March 1972, 3rd revised and enlarged edition (2 volumes) (Iyengar).

Kar, Nalinikanta, *Notes* preserved in Jatin Mukherjee Papers, at the Nehru Museum, New Delhi; published in *Bagha Jatin*, by Prithwindra Mukherjee, Dey's Publishing, 1990 (1st Edition).

Majumdar, Bimanbehari, *Militant Nationalism in India*, General Printers & Publishers, Calcutta, 1966.

Morley to Minto, *Letters*, Vol. I (d/ 11 May 1906), Vol. II (d/ 28 August 1907; 5 December 1907), quoted in *India under Morley and Minto*, by M.N. Das, George Allen & Unwin, London, 1964.

Mukherjee, Prithwindra, « Swamiji–Nivedita–Jatin Mukherjee » in (BNJS), Vol. II, 1966.

Mukherjee, Prithwindra, *Undying Courage*, Academic Publishers, Calcutta, 1991.

Mukherjee, Prithwindra, *Bagha Jatin*, National Book Trust, New Delhi, 2010.

Mukherjee, Prithwindra, "Le patriotisme, une religion\: Swami Vivekananda" in *Les racines intellectuelles du mouvement d'indépendance de l'Inde (1893-1918)*, Editions Codex, 2010, France.

Mukhopadhyay, Jadugopal, *Biplabi jiban'er smriti*, 1956, Calcutta (2nd Edition).

Pal, Bipinchandra, *Navayug'er bangala*, Bipinchandra Parishad, Calcutta, 1964 (PAL).

Roy, M.N., "Jatindranath Mukherjee" in *Independent India*, February 27, 1949; reprinted in *Men I Met*, Bombay, 1968.

Samanta, Amiya K (compiled by), *Terrorism in Bengal*, Government of West Bengal, 1995, 6 Vol. (TIB).

Sarkar, Benoy Kumar, foreword to *The Social Philosophy of Vivekananda* by Trilochan Das, Cooperative Book Depot, Calcutta, 1949.

Swami Vivekananda, *Complete Works*, Mayavati Memorial Edition, Advaita Ashram, 1926-37 (7 Volumes) (CWSV).

Swami Vivekananda, *vani o rachana*, Udbodhan Office, Calcutta, Vol. II.

Swami Vivekananda, *Les yogas pratiques*, translated into French by Jean Herbert, Albin Michel, Paris, 1970.

Tagore, Rabindranath, *Rabindra-rachanabali*, Visvabharati, Calcutta, 2000, 17 Vol. (RNT).

About the Author

Dr. Prithwindra Mukherjee was born in Calcutta (1936) and brought up in Pondicherry (1948-66). He taught languages and literature at Sri Aurobindo International Centre of Education (1955-66). He moved to Paris when he received the French Government Scholarship (1966-70). His first thesis was on Sri Aurobindo at the Sorbonne University (1970). Later, he taught at two Paris faculties (1974-81). He received the Fulbright Scholarship for research in the United States. In 1981, he joined the French National Centre of Scientific Research. His thesis for the State Doctorate on pre-Gandhian Freedom movement in British India was supervised by Raymond Aron (1974-1982) and was published with a foreword by Jacques Attali. He has authored many books and other publications on diverse subjects.

Honours and Awards

French composer Henri Dutilleux's *Correspondances* opus for voice and orchestra (Berlin Philharmoniker, 2003; Deutsche Grammophon, 2012), contains as the first movement Prithwindra Mukherjee's "Danse cosmique" in homage to Shiva Nataraja. Dr. Mukherjee's poem on Shiva Nataraja has been translated into twelve languages of the world. The French Ministry of Culture has conferred on Dr. Prithwindra Mukherjee the rank of Chevalier (Knight) in the Order of Arts and Letters, in 2009. The French Academy has conferred on him its prestigious Hirayama Award in 2014.

Publications

In addition to 12 LPs and 2 documentary films (CNRS), Dr. Prithwindra Mukherjee has published more than 60 books and 400 articles in Bengali, French and English. He is a pioneering translator from French into Bengali, and from Bengali into French for UNESCOand other publishers, and is founder-member of the Association of French Literary Translators. He is referred to as "the delicious Franco-Bengali poet" by the *Figaro Littéraire* (1974) for his *Poèmes du Bangladesh.* Some of his prominent works include *French Anthology of a Thousand Years of Bengali Poetry* (1991, Pocket edition 1992) (Anthologie de la poésiebengalie); *The Cognitive Study of the Scales of Indian Music*, with a Foreword by Pandit Ravi Shankar (2003) (Thât/Mélakartâ: Les échellesfondamentales de la musiqueindienne du Nord et du Sud); *BaghaJatin: Life and Times of Jatindranath Mukherjee* (National Book Trust, 2010) launched by H.E. Pranab Mukherjee, the then Finance Minister; *A Shade Sharp, A Shade Flat*: a trilingual anthology with 108 poems by Rabindranath Tagore, launched by the President of the Société des Gens de Lettres, Paris; *Les raciness intellectuelles du movement d'indépendance de l'Inde (1893-1918)*, PhD thesis on the pre-Gandhian freedom movement in India, Editions Codex (Foreword: Jacques Attali); and *Le Spontané*: a study of the *sahaja-yâna* quest through the 8th century *Caryâ-pada* and the contemporary *Bâul* songs, Almora Publishers, Paris.

ABOUT INDUS SOURCE BOOKS

We are a niche, independent publishing house passionately committed to publishing good and relevant literature. Although our primary focus is publishing books on spirituality and philosophy, we also publish general non-fiction in diverse genres. We seek to provide positive, spiritual insights for harmony and better living. Through our publications we would like to share the received wisdom, lighting the way for fellow-travellers. We are committed to our goal of promoting understanding of the Self, between faiths and cultures, and of the world in which we live.

Visit our website www.indussource.com for more details.

Indus Source Books
PO Box 6194
Malabar Hill PO
Mumbai 400006
India
www.indussource.com
info@indussource.com